Understanding Your Child's Brain

Understanding Your Child's Brain simplifies the neuroscience behind what is going on in a child's brain during the first six years of life to help parents develop the full intellectual and emotional potential of their children.

The book starts with an accessible explanation of the pillars and principals to understanding the child's brain. It then provides tools to help parents communicate more effectively with, nurture empathy in, and enforce rules and positive behaviours for their children. Examining how to develop the emotional intelligence of children as well as their intellect, the chapters examine how to raise children based on trust, assertiveness, and fearlessness, while also providing support and exercises in improving language, memory, creativity, and self-control.

This book offers parents and educators practical solutions to parenting problems and realistic advice for ensuring the healthy emotional and intellectual development of their children. It will also be relevant to all mental health professionals who want to be more assertive when talking to parents about their child's problems and growth.

Álvaro Bilbao, PhD, is a psychotherapist, doctor in psychology, neuropsychology, and father to three children. Trained at Johns Hopkins Hospital and the Kennedy Krieger Institute, he has also collaborated with the World Health Organization.

T0384236

'*Understanding Your Child's Brain* includes common sense, easy to understand tools and strategies that are grounded in science to help parents and educators manage the everyday challenges encountered when raising and teaching children. Throughout the book, Dr. Bilbao explains principles of psychology, child development, and neuroscience to help the reader understand not just how to interact more positively and effectively with children but also why the techniques described facilitate healthy psychological and neurological development. This book absolutely will help parents to more fully understand their child's brain.'

Beth Slomine, *Director, Neuropsychological Rehabilitation Services, Kennedy Krieger Institute, Baltimore*

'A book all adults should read.'

Javier Ortigosa, *Psychotherapist, Spain*

'In this well written and easy to read book for parents, Álvaro Bilbao, PhD, a neuropsychologist and father of three, gives insight into how a child's early brain development shapes their world and affects their learning and behavior. Drawing on years of clinical practice and sound neuroscience, Dr. Bilbao provides parents with practical, age-appropriate strategies for everyday life to foster a child's intellectual and emotional growth to help them reach their full potential. I highly recommend this book to all those raising young children.'

Margaret B. Pulsifer, *PhD, Massachusetts General Hospital, Harvard Medical School*

Understanding Your Child's Brain

Álvaro Bilbao

Routledge
Taylor & Francis Group

LONDON AND NEW YORK

Designed cover image: © Getty Image

First English edition published 2023
by Routledge
4 Park Square, Milton Park, Abingdon, Oxon, OX14 4RN

and by Routledge
605 Third Avenue, New York, NY 10158

Routledge is an imprint of the Taylor & Francis Group, an informa business

© 2023 Álvaro Bilbao

The right of Álvaro Bilbao to be identified as author of this
work has been asserted in accordance with sections 77 and 78
of the Copyright, Designs and Patents Act 1988.

All rights reserved. No part of this book may be reprinted
or reproduced or utilised in any form or by any electronic,
mechanical, or other means, now known or hereafter invented,
including photocopying and recording, or in any information
storage or retrieval system, without permission in writing from
the publishers.

Trademark notice: Product or corporate names may be
trademarks or registered trademarks and are used only for
identification and explanation without intent to infringe.

First Spanish edition published by Plataforma Editorial S. L. 2015

British Library Cataloguing-in Publication Data
A catalogue record for this book is available from the British Library

Library of Congress Cataloging-in-Publication Data
Names: Bilbao, Álvaro, 1976– author.
Title: Understanding your child's brain / Álvaro Bilbao.
Other titles: Cerebro del niño explicado a los padres. English
Description: First English edition. | New York, NY : Routledge,
2023. | Includes index. |
Identifiers: LCCN 2022046666 (print) | LCCN 2022046667
(ebook) | ISBN 9781032418599 (hbk) | ISBN 9781032418582
(pbk) | ISBN 9781003360117 (ebk)
Subjects: LCSH: Child psychology. | Child rearing. |
Learning, Psychology of. | Educational psychology. | Pediatric
neuropsychology. | Brain—Growth.
Classification: LCC BF721 .B4243 2023 (print) | LCC BF721
(ebook) | DDC 155.4—dc23/eng/20230206
LC record available at https://lccn.loc.gov/2022046666
LC ebook record available at https://lccn.loc.gov/2022046667

ISBN: 978-1-032-41859-9 (hbk)
ISBN: 978-1-032-41858-2 (pbk)
ISBN: 978-1-003-36011-7 (ebk)

DOI: 10.4324/9781003360117

Typeset in Times New Roman
by codeMantra

In memory of Tristán, who, wherever he is, spends his days laughing with his parents and playing with his siblings and cousins.

Contents

Acknowledgements   ix

Introduction: The child's brain explained to parents   1

PART I
Fundamentals   7

1 Principles for full brain development   9

2 Your child is like a tree   10

3 Enjoy the moment   14

4 The Top 3: What every parent needs to know about the brain   18

5 Balance   24

PART II
Tools   27

6 Tools for supporting brain development   29

7 Patience and understanding   31

8 Empathy   38

9 Reinforcing rules and positive behaviour   46

10 Alternatives to punishment   57

11 Establishing limits without drama   64

12 Communication   72

PART III
Emotional intelligence   **77**

13 Teach emotional intelligence   79

14 Bonds   81

15 Confidence   88

16 Growing up without fear   96

17 Assertiveness   103

18 Sowing the seeds for happiness   111

PART IV
Strengthen the intellectual brain   **117**

19 Intellectual development   119

20 Attention   123

21 Memory   130

22 Language   137

23 Visual intelligence   144

24 Self-control   150

25 Creativity   156

26 The best apps for children under six years of age   163

27 Farewell   164

Index   167

Acknowledgements

I would like to thank my parents and my parents-in-law for their incredible work as parents, which now extends to their grandchildren. Similarly, to my brother, brothers and sisters-in-law, aunts, uncles, grandparents and cousins. Together they make up that essential band of people who are needed to care for a child.

I must give my sincerest thanks and recognition to all teachers, who relentlessly support the development of children in every corner of the world. I can't imagine a more important job in society than that of caring for the greatest treasures of the present, while promoting the greatest promises of the future. Their experience brings out the best in each child where parents are more likely to lose their way, their enthusiasm awakens the desire to learn things in a way that parents cannot, and their patience and tenderness embrace our children when the parents are not there. Above all, my own children's teachers: Amaya, Ana Belén, Elena, Jesús and Sonia, and to my former teachers: Rosa, Marili and Javier.

And of course to my wife, Paloma, and my three wonderful children: Diego, Leire and Lucía. Even though I have been studying the human brain my entire life, these four people are the ones who have given meaning to my knowledge and who have taught me everything I know about the wonderful world of a child's brain.

Introduction

The child's brain explained to parents

The most important period of life is not the age of university studies, but the first one, the period from birth to the age of six.

Maria Montessori

Children awaken unique emotions in any adult. Their gestures, their genuine joy and their innocence move us in a way that no other experience in life can. The child connects directly with a very special part of us: the child that we were, and still are. Perhaps you have once felt the desire to sing in the street, have an argument with your boss or jump into a puddle on a rainy day. Yet because of responsibilities, or embarrassment, you have chosen not to. Being with a child is a beautiful experience, because when we are with them, we connect with a very special part of ourselves: the lost child that we need to make contact with at so many moments of our life, and which is possibly the best part of each one of us.

If you have this book in your hands it is because, as a father, mother, educator or healthcare professional there is a child in your life. Therefore, you have the opportunity to connect with the part of your brain that laughs, plays and dreams within you. Educating a child is also a great responsibility and possibly the most momentous act in many people's lives. The transcendence of parenthood reaches all levels of human existence. On a biological level, children are the seed that spreads your genes and ensures your transcendence through future generations. On a psychological level, for many people it implies the realisation of an uncontrollable instinct. And on a spiritual level, it represents the possibility of achieving fulfilment by seeing happy children grow up.

As any parent understands at that moment in which they hold their child in their arms for the first time, being a parent also carries a series of different responsibilities. First, those which involve caring for the child, including nutrition, grooming and basic protection. Fortunately, hospital midwives and the ever-willing grandmothers will have given you theoretical and practical classes on all of this. Secondly, there are the economic responsibilities.

DOI: 10.4324/9781003360117-1

A child comes with a series of costs that must be borne, to the delight of department stores, pharmacies, nurseries and supermarkets. Fortunately, for an average of twelve years, the education system has taught you so that you can earn a salary. You can read and write. You can work a computer. You can speak – or attempt to speak – another language. You are able to sit for almost eight hours every day. You know how to work in a team and have specific training in whatever it is you do. The third responsibility of every parent, and the most important one, is that of educating their children. From my perspective, education is nothing more than supporting the child in their brain development, so that one day that brain allows them to be autonomous, achieve their goals and feel good about themselves. Although, by explaining it in this way, it may appear simple. Educating has its complications, and most parents do not receive any training on how they can help their children during this process. Essentially, they do not understand what basic brain functioning is, how it develops, or how they can support its growth. On occasion, every parent will feel lost, lose direction or feel insecure about how they can help their children in different aspects of their intellectual and emotional growth. At other times, they will act with confidence, but in a way that goes against what their child's brain needs at that time.

I don't want to misguide you, or give you a distorted idea on the influence that, as a parent, you can have on the intellectual and emotional development of your children. Your son or daughter comes as standard, with a character that will mark their way of being for the rest of their lives. Some children are more introverted and others more extroverted. There are calm children and others who are excitable. Likewise, we know that at least 50% of your child's intelligence is determined by their genes. Some studies indicate that possibly another 25% depends on their classmates and the friends with whom they socialise. This has led some experts to assume that parents barely influence their children's development. However, this statement is not correct. The child, especially during their first years of life, needs their parents in order to develop. Without your care and the words or hands to support and calm them down, the child would grow up with irreparable emotional and intellectual deficiencies. It is in the safety, care and stimulation offered by the family that all the child's brain development rests.

Today, mums and dads have more opportunities than at any other time in history to get it right with their children. We have more information, and research about the brain provides us with the knowledge and practical tools that can help our children to fully develop. Unfortunately, we also have more opportunities to make mistakes. The reality is that, in just two decades, the number of children taking neurological or psychiatric medication in the United States has increased sevenfold. This trend continues to rise and seems to be spreading like wildfire through the "developed" world and, today, one in nine children will spend part of their school years under the influence of psychotropic drugs. The reality is that we have lost the values of children's education, values that science indicates as being fundamental for a balanced brain development. As a consequence, in the fields of education and child development, there is a rise in corporations interested in making money through complex brain stimulation programmes, nursery schools that are capable of creating geniuses, or drugs that reverse the possibility of becoming distracted and improve behaviour. These companies operate under the popular belief that such programmes, stimulation or treatments have a positive impact on brain development. At the other end of the scale there are other theories, where there are parents who rely on a radically natural education, in which the child grows up free from rules or frustration. They are encouraged by studies that show that frustration in a baby can cause emotional problems, that limits interfere with a child's creative potential, or that an excess of rewards can undermine a child's confidence. Both approaches, firstly, that the child's brain is improved through the use of technology and, secondly, that the human being is only able to achieve full development through exploration and free experience, have shown to be incorrect. The reality is that the brain does not work as we would like it to work, nor sometimes how we think it works. The brain works in the way that it does.

Neuroscientists around the world have for decades been trying to decipher the principles that support brain development and what are the most effective strategies in helping children to be happier and to enjoy their full intellectual capabilities. Research on evolution and genetics reveals that, far from being purely kind, human beings have opposing instincts. It is enough to go to a school playground to see how, far from the eyes of the teachers, instincts of generosity appear in the form of altruism and mutual collaboration, but also other negative instincts, such as aggressiveness and domination. Without the support of parents and teachers to guide the child, helping them to meet their own needs within the limits established by respect for others, the child would be lost. We know that our ability to transmit values and culture from generation to generation is what has greatly helped our species to evolve, making us more civilised and supportive – although, in these times, it may not seem this way; it is a job that the brain cannot do on its own and that needs the attentive work of parents and teachers.

Other research on brain development provides data which shows that early stimulation has no impact on the intelligence of a healthy child. In this sense, the only thing that seems to be proven is that, during the first years of life, the child has a greater capacity to develop what we understand as a perfect pitch, or the ability to learn music or a language as if it were their mother tongue. This is not to say that a bilingual school is better than a non-bilingual school, particularly since if the teachers are not native, the child will develop the language with an accent, rather than a perfect pitch. In this sense, it may be more beneficial for children to watch films in the original version, as happens in other countries, or that they have a few classes a week in a foreign language such as Chinese, but taught by native teachers. Furthermore, we know that programmes like Baby Einstein, or listening to music from Mozart, do not contribute to the child's intellectual development either. A child who listens to classical music can relax, and a few minutes later can perform certain concentration exercises more effectively, but nothing more. After a few minutes, the effect dissipates. We also have strong data that shows that children's exposure to smartphones, tablets and other electronic devices raises the risk of behavioural problems or attention deficit disorders. This data also indicates that the deficit is undoubtedly over diagnosed; in other words, there is a relatively high percentage of children taking psychiatric medication that they do not actually need. The tendency to over diagnose attention deficit is only the tip of the iceberg. Far from taking responsibility for it, pharmaceutical companies merely take advantage of the educational context of many homes. The lengthy working hours, a lack of dedication from the parents, a lack of patience and of limits and – as we have already pointed out – the emergence of smartphones and tablets, seem to be, at least in part, behind the huge increase in cases of attention deficit disorder and childhood depression.

There are countless miracle programmes that promise to develop child intelligence, but as you can see, when these programmes are subjected to scientific rigour, they do not show any signs of efficacy. Possibly the reason for the failure of so many of them is that their main interest is to accelerate the natural process of brain development, with the idea that developing sooner allows you to develop further. However, brain development is not a process that can be accelerated without losing some of its properties. In the same way that a genetically modified tomato, which ripens in a few days and achieves the "ideal" dimensions and colour, loses the essence of its flavour, a brain that develops under pressure, hurrying to skip stages, can lose part of its essence along the way. Empathy, the ability to wait, feelings of calm or love, cannot be cultivated at a greenhouse pace. They require slow growth and patient progenitors who know how to wait for the child to bear its best fruits, just at the moment they are ready to do so. This is the reason why the most important findings in neuroscience regarding the development of the child's brain grind to a halt at seemingly simple aspects, such as the positive influence of fruit and fish intake during pregnancy, and during the first years of the child's life; the psychological benefits of cradling the baby in your arms; the role of affection in the child's intellectual development; or the importance of conversations between mother and child in the development of memory and language, in clear acknowledgement that in brain development, essential elements are crucial.

The truth is that we know many things about the brain that could help parents, but which unfortunately they don't know about. I want to help you understand how you can influence your child's brain development in a very positive way. There are hundreds of studies that show that the brain has enormous plasticity, and that parents who use the right strategies can help their children have a balanced brain development. This is why I have gathered the fundamentals, tools and techniques that can help you be the best influence in the intellectual and emotional development of your own child. With that, you will not only be able to help them develop good intellectual and emotional skills, but you will also contribute to preventing difficulties in their development, such as attention deficit, childhood depression or behavioural problems. I am convinced that basic knowledge about how a child's brain develops and builds itself can be a great help for those parents who want to take advantage of them. I trust that the knowledge, strategies and experiences that you will find below will contribute to making your work as a parent a deeply satisfactory experience. But above all, I hope that by delving into the wonderful world of the child's brain, you will be able to connect with the lost child within you, and better understand your own children in order to get the best out of each and every one of you.

Part I

Fundamentals

1

Principles for full brain development

The intelligent have plans; the wise have principles.

(Raheel Farooq)

A principle is a universal and necessary condition that allows us to explain and understand the world around us. The law of gravity is a basic principle of astronomy, hygiene is a basic principle of health, and mutual trust, for example, is a basic principle of friendship. As with any task given to a human being, a child's education also features some basic principles that will allow any parent to understand what they have to do in most situations; furthermore, how they can use these principles to weigh up any alternatives they come across in their education and upbringing.

As with any parent, you have already faced, and will continue to face, many dilemmas during the long process of your children growing up. They can be specific and practical issues, such as the choice between scolding your child and being patient, or deciding whether to wait for them to finish their plate versus allowing them to leave their food. But there can also be broader, almost philosophical issues, such as choosing a school for them, deciding to opt for extracurricular activities or taking a stand regarding time spent in front of the television or playing with a mobile phone. In reality, all decisions, philosophical and seemingly inconsequential, will condition the development of your child's brain. Therefore it is helpful to settle on clear, practical and solid principles.

In this first part of the book, I will introduce you to the basic principles of child brain development that every parent should know with four simple and easy-to-remember ideas for you to understand – the four main strands on which to build your job of educating the intellectual and emotional brain of your child. These are the principles on which I have based my own children's upbringing, and which guide me when I am faced with any decision regarding their education. I am certain that if you keep these principles in mind on a day-to-day basis and when any doubts arise over the education and parenting of your children, you will make the right decision.

DOI: 10.4324/9781003360117-3

2

Your child is like a tree

If you plan on being anything less than you are capable of being, you will probably be unhappy all the days of your life.

(Attributed to Abraham Maslow)

Perhaps you have thought at some point about how a newborn foal or fawn tries to stand up on its own legs. After a few minutes they can stand up and take their first, trembling steps behind their mother. For a human being, whose offspring take about a year to take their first steps – and in some cases forty until they leave their parents' house – watching this performance can be fascinating. The newborn human being's need for protection is absolute. No other mammal needs as much protection as the human baby. This means that in the minds of many parents, their child is a fragile and dependent being. Although this is the case during the first year of life, and in a practical sense during the subsequent years, I would like you to come to the end of this chapter with the idea that your child is essentially the same as a fawn, zebra or foal you see trying to stand up shortly after birth.

A baby is certainly not able to follow behind its parents when they leave the hospital after birth. However, babies can do something equally as fascinating. If the newborn baby is placed on top of the mother's womb just after she gives birth, far from keeping still, they will begin to move along her skin until they can see the dark spot of the mother's nipple. They will continue to climb until they can latch on to it. If you have also had the privilege of witnessing this, you will agree with me that it is an incredible scene for any parent. However, it is also completely natural. Every human being is programmed with the drive needed to seize their autonomy and happiness. The idea that human beings have a natural tendency to develop themselves fully is a well-extended and accepted premise in the world of psychology and education. It is also a

DOI: 10.4324/9781003360117-4

basic principle of biology: all living beings have a natural tendency to grow and develop themselves fully. In fertile soil, with minimum light and water, the seed of an oak will grow at an unstoppable rate, thickening and stretching its trunk, unfolding its branches and opening its leaves until it reaches the size and majesty of an adult oak. In the same way, a bird will grow feathers, gain strength in its wings and skill in its beak to fly, catch worms, and build its own nest, and a blue whale will grow to become the biggest living thing on the planet. If nothing prevents it, all living things in nature have a natural tendency to reach their full potential.

Your child does too. The first to recognise this principle were the psychologists of the "humanist" wave, towards the middle of the 20th century. At that time, psychology was debated among two great schools of thought: psychoanalysis, which mainly defended the idea that the human being was conditioned by unconscious desires and needs; and behaviourism, which highlighted the role of rewards and punishments in determining our behaviours and our own happiness. Abraham Maslow, the father of humanistic psychology, supported the view that the human being, like other living beings, has a natural tendency towards full development. In the case of the cherry tree, that full development translates into the yearly blossoms in April, and in offering sweet and delicious fruit; in the case of the cheetah, fully developing means running faster than any other land animal, and in the case of the squirrel it means being able to build a drey and collect nuts for the winter.

For the human being, reaching its potential carries connotations that imply a greater evolution than that of plants or animals, although the principle of development is the same. Because your child has a complex brain, allowing him or her to feel and think, develop social relationships and achieve goals, by nature they need little more than what a bird would need. The human brain shows a natural tendency to feel good about itself and other people, to seek happiness and to find meaning in their existence. Psychologists call this ultimate goal of every human being, "self-fulfilment", and we know that every person, if the necessary conditions are met, tends towards it. Steven Pinker, one of the neuroscientists to have studied the evolution of our brain in more depth, ensures that the struggle for life, the desire for freedom and the search for happiness form part of our DNA. According to Maslow, for a human being, reaching our potential means feeling good around other people, feeling good about ourselves and reaching a state of harmony and complete satisfaction. Maslow illustrated this trend towards development using a hierarchy of basic needs that I'm sure you already know. I wanted to share this version, aimed at the needs of small children, with you.

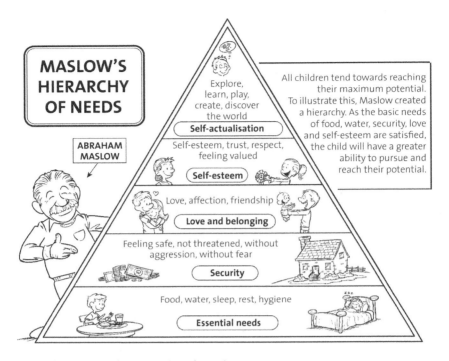

Figure 2.1 Maslow's hierarchy of needs

As the picture illustrates, just as a tree needs minimal conditions to grow and develop – essentially, some firm soil, water, sunlight and space to grow –, your child's brain also has a few basic requirements. For the human being, firm soil, the first level, would be the equivalent of the physical security afforded by receiving the basic needs of food, rest and hygiene while growing up, as well as a safe environment at home that is free from threats or abuse, which corresponds to the second level. The third level, "watering" the brain in order for it to grow, is nothing more than the warmth of affectionate parents who emotionally protect and nourish the child and allow them to achieve a healthy amount of self-esteem. Fourth, in the same way that the tree needs space to develop, the child needs trust and freedom from their parents, otherwise their talent and desire to explore can end up stifled by insecurity and lack of space granted by their parents. Finally, just as the branches of the tree stretch to reach the sun's rays, the child's brain naturally seeks stimuli that allow them to explore, play, experience and discover the world of objects and people who surround them, in search of their full development.

In the chapters of this book we will explore these four basic but essential conditions for full brain development. In this chapter, however, I would like to emphasise the importance of trust. Remember that your child is like a tree, programmed to grow and develop fully. Neither teachers, nor parents, nor your own child, yet know what kind of tree they will become. Over the years, you will discover if your child is a commanding sequoia, a solitary poplar, a cherry tree full of fruit, a sturdy palm tree, or a majestic oak. What you can trust in, however, is that your child's brain is programmed to fully develop and reach its full potential. In many cases, your only job will be precisely that: trust.

3

Enjoy the moment

"Tempus fugit" or "It escapes, irretrievable time"

(Virgil)

About five years ago I was rushing to catch the train that takes me to work every day, when I came across our butcher. With a broad smile on his face, he said: "Good morning! How are you getting on?" By that time, I had started to take my son to nursery every morning. I woke up an hour earlier than usual to get ready before he woke up. Although I had always dreamt of having a family, and I loved children, the truth is that I felt overwhelmed by my new responsibilities and the loss of freedom, as is the case with many first-time parents. At that time, the effort I had to make was the equivalent of waking up twice, dressing twice, having breakfast twice, and going to work twice. It was a drastic change from my previous life, in which I only had to take care of myself. I was tired, out of place and, in a sense, unhappy. Consequently, I responded to the butcher, complaining about my tiredness and lamenting my lack of time. He, older and therefore wiser than me, gave me advice that I will never forget: "With children, time passes, and it only passes once. What you stop doing now will never come back. You will lose it forever." At that moment, somehow, something in my brain clicked. I woke up.

Enjoy parenthood

Being a parent is much more than a responsibility. It's a privilege. I often hear from fathers who, like me on that third day of nursery, see their paternity as a burden. They bemoan the loss of their freedom, their exhaustion, or the frustration involved in raising a child, and they seem to forget the enjoyment that can come from being a father. Being a parent undoubtedly means giving up many things, or postponing them, such as your free time, travelling, your career, or getting some rest; they all get put on the back burner. Any parent knows that having a child means going from living a carefree life to suddenly having a very, very busy life. In my view, giving all

DOI: 10.4324/9781003360117-5

this up only makes sense if it is compensated for in other ways. With children, the greatest compensation is enjoyment.

If you are often overwhelmed by the responsibility of caring for your children, I know this can be hard but I want you to try to redirect your attention to something more positive. When the brain changes its focus of attention, it can see things in a completely different way. Look at this drawing.

It was drawn in 1915 and shows a wife and a mother-in-law (the original title is *My Wife and My Mother-in Law*, by W. E. Hill). Are you able to see both? The curious thing about the drawing is that, depending on where in the picture you focus your attention, it will look like a young woman or an old woman. If you look at the part of the drawing where the coat lapels meet, you will see a prominent chin and the drawing will look like an old woman. If, on the other hand, you focus your attention on the part of the face that is just beneath the hat, you will see the silhouette of a young woman with her head tilted. Elderly woman, or young woman. Mother-in-law, or wife. The reality is that both exist simultaneously in the drawing, but you cannot see them at the same time. In a sense, the experience of raising a child is similar to this picture. You can spend a lifetime paying attention to the bitter face of sacrifice, or focus on the beauty of watching your children grow up.

Carrying your sleeping son to bed means that he feels completely safe in your arms. Being late for work because you have stopped to pick up pinecones on the way to school means that that morning you have been able to savour a magical moment with your daughter. Having a sleepless night because your little one's teeth are coming through means that you are with him when he is having a bad time. Giving up a day of work to attend a school event means that you are there for the important moments of her life. Undoubtedly, there will be hard times. But if you want to go beyond survival and have a full and satisfying experience as a parent, I suggest you try to turn your attention to the beautiful side of parenthood and enjoy it with all your energy.

Seizing the moment

As Maria Montessori's quote in the introduction to this book states, the first six years are the most important in your child's life. During these years, we develop a sense of security, both in ourselves and the world around us, our language develops, the way we learn is determined, and the foundations to allow us to resolve problems in the future are set.

In this sense, it is very important that you take advantage of your child's first years of life to be with them and help them develop their cognitive and emotional abilities. This does not mean enrolling your child in complex early stimulation programmes or taking them to the best nursery in your area. For every game you play, every cry they make, every walk you go on together and every bottle of milk they drink, there is a chance to educate and enhance the brain development of your children. Far from school and even further from extracurricular activities, we know that during these first years of life, parents and siblings are the ones that will have the most influence on their development and evolution. The values, rules, insight, memory and ability to face up to problems are transmitted through language, games, large and small gestures, and all the other details – which are seemingly small – that shape their education. The aim of this book is to give you tools and strategies that you can use in your day-to-day life; tools that allow your child to learn without any pressure, through play and enjoyment. In a natural way that helps build a satisfactory and lasting relationship between you.

Enjoying the moment

If all those people who are determined to get the most out of life use the motto: "Seize the day" ("*Carpe diem*"), all those who want to help their children achieve their full potential, should use: "Enjoy the moment." Enjoyment should be a basic part of a child's development. The reason is very simple: adults perceive the world through ideas, words and reasoning, but have you ever stopped to think how your children perceive the world? Not all living beings perceive the universe around them in the same way. For example, the dog's brain perceives the world through smells; bats, through noises that collide with their sonar; and bees, through electromagnetic impulses. In the same way, the child, especially during the first years of life, perceives the world in a completely different way than you do. The child perceives the world primarily through emotions, play and affection.

In this sense, playing is fundamental in supporting the intellectual and emotional development of the child. Clearly the child can also learn from parents who seldom play, but playing offers many advantages. The child's brain is designed to learn through play. When we play with a child, they go into learning mode; all their senses are focused on the activity, they are able to stay concentrated, watch your gestures and your words, and recall them much better than if we instruct or direct them. When we play with a child, we come into emotional contact with them; the game itself awakens their emotions, but also the physical contact with their parent, who holds them, hugs them or nibbles them as part of the game. When a child plays, they are able to take on a role, put themselves in the place of someone else and think about the future. When a child plays, they are capable of thinking and acting with greater intelligence and maturity than their own age, because the game expands their mind like no other activity. If you want to get into your child's world and work from their perspective, I recommend that you sit or lie on the floor and be at their level. There is no better way to get a child's attention. I can assure you, that without saying a word, any child in the room will approach you, eager to play, happy because you are coming closer to their world of emotions and play. I invite you to sit in the front row of your children's lives. This is why in this chapter, and throughout the book, I'm going to suggest that you sit on the carpet and use play and fun as educational tools. From a place as low down as the floor of your house, you will have the most privileged platform from which to observe and participate in your child's brain development. Enjoy it!

4

The Top 3

What every parent needs to know about the brain

Investment in knowledge pays the best interest.

(Benjamin Franklin)

I know first-hand that having basic knowledge about how the brain works and develops can be tremendously practical for guiding parents in the education of their children. You don't have to be a neuroscientist. Four general observations are enough for you to understand some fundamental ideas that can help you make decisions and guide the process of your child's education. Throughout the book you will find useful and practical information to help your child develop their full potential. In this chapter we will open the doors to the unknown world of the brain, so you can learn the Top 3; what every parent should know in order to start helping their child realise their full potential. There are three very simple ideas that you will be able to understand and remember perfectly

1: Connection

At birth, a baby has almost all of the one hundred billion neurons he or she will have when they are older. The main difference between the child's brain and that of the adult is that these neurons will have developed trillions of connections with each other. We call each of these connections "synapses". To give you an idea of the incredible capacity for brain interconnection, bear in mind that these connections can be created in just two seconds, and that some neurons can connect with another five hundred thousand neighbouring neurons.

What is more interesting than these numbers, is the fact that each of these connections can be translated into a new piece of knowledge that the child's brain has acquired. The position, strength and direction of the thumb when grabbing their favourite dinosaur are reflected in the child's brain through different neural connections, and also through the feeling

DOI: 10.4324/9781003360117-6

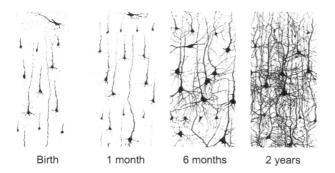

| Birth | 1 month | 6 months | 2 years |

Figure 4.1 Neuronal connectivity at birth, 1 month, 6 months, 2 years

that, when they concentrate, they can achieve what they want. When you talk to your child, when you kiss them, or simply when they look at you, their brain makes connections to help them to face life as an adult. I will teach you how to connect with your child, so they can make valuable connections which allow them to achieve their goals and feel good about themselves. We will devote an entire chapter to learning how you can help your child create valuable connections more effectively. But for now, I am only going to ask you to remember that everything you teach your child will be recorded in the form of a connection, which will most likely accompany them throughout their life.

2: Reason and intuition

Point two of the Top 3 will help you to broaden your understanding of your child's intelligence, and help them to increase their self-confidence. The outermost part of the brain, which we also call "cerebral cortex", is divided into two hemispheres: the left and the right. The left hemisphere controls the movements of the right hand and is the dominant one in most people. Among the functions of this hemisphere, is the ability to speak, read or write, to remember people's names, to exercise self-control and to show proactiveness and optimism in life. We could say that this hemisphere has a rational, logical, positive and controlling character. The right hemisphere controls the left hand and, as often happens with this hand, its intellectual activity tends to be less noticeable. As you will see, however, its functions are equally important. This hemisphere represents and interprets nonverbal language, it forms quick, general impressions, it takes a comprehensive view and is able to detect small errors and correct them on the spur of the moment. Its character is more intuitive, artistic and emotional.

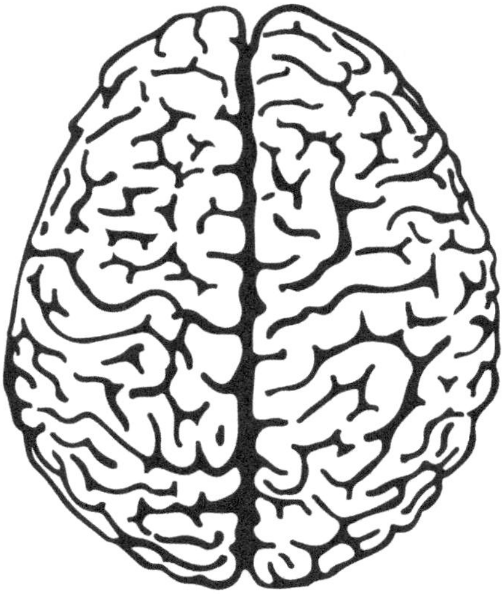

Left hemisphere	**Right hemisphere**
Establish rules and systems	Give sense to the parts
Logical thinking	Intuitive thinking
Language	Creativity
Reflective	Emotional
Science	Music
Reason	Art

Figure 4.2 Main left vs right hemisphere functions

With this differentiation I do not mean that right-handed people are more intuitive and left-handed people are more logical (no such differences have been found). Additionally, I would not want you to think that children can be either intuitive or rational. In fact, we know that all people need the functions of the two hemispheres to have full brain development. A painter needs to have a good overall view – right hemisphere – but also needs good control of each of his strokes – left hemisphere. In the same way, a lawyer needs to remember many written laws – left hemisphere – but also needs to support the general meaning that asserts them – right hemisphere. Throughout the last part of the book you will learn how to support the brain development of the different parts represented in the two hemispheres, but, more importantly, you will also be able to understand how each of them influences the emotional development of the child.

3: Three brains in one

Now I'm going to share with you what is possibly the most useful piece of data that every parent can have about their children's brains. The human brain has evolved over millions of years from the most primitive of life forms, into the most complex work of creation. Many people believe that the outcome of all this evolution is a brain that is more able to reason. However, reality differs from this concept of the brain as a cold, calculating organ.

Throughout these millions of years, the brain has been creating structures to enable it to find food, avoid danger, seek safety and lastly, communicate and solve complex problems effectively. All this evolution is reflected in a brain that, instead of emerging as something different, has been updating itself, incorporating new skills and tools, in addition to those it already had. The different phases of this evolution are reflected in the brain's own configuration, allowing us to differentiate between the older structures, which are highly specialised in processing emotions, and the more modern ones, which are capable of complex intellectual calculations. From my point of view you cannot educate a child without focusing on the education of the different levels or steps that shape the child's brain.

A metaphor that helps in the understanding of the different stages and structures that make up the human brain, is that of having three brains in one.

The reptilian brain is the most primitive of all and is located at the base. It is the brain that we share with reptiles and the one that enables us to fight for survival. In this brain there are structures that make our heart beat and allow us to breathe, others that regulate states of alertness (being awake or asleep), and more that let us detect temperature changes and provoke the feeling of hunger.

On the second level we have a series of structures that we call the emotional brain. This brain was developed during the time of the first mammals and its function is based on the ability to distinguish between pleasant and unpleasant emotions. It is therefore activated when unpleasant sensations (dangers, threats and situations that cause us fear) need to be avoided and when in search and pursuit of pleasant emotions (feeding ourselves, being with people who make us feel safe and who give us love).

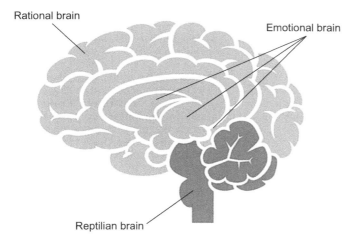

Figure 4.3 Rational brain Emotional brain Reptilian brain

In the final step, the most evolved, is the superior or rational brain – that which distinguishes humans from other animals and allows us to have self-awareness, to communicate, reason, place ourselves in other people's shoes or to make decisions based on more logical or intuitive thinking.

As you can see, far from being just a cold and rational organ, the human brain is an organ of reason, with feelings and emotions. In fact, in a child it is the reptilian and emotional brains that are in control. Until they reach the age of one, parents should interact primarily with the child's primitive brain. At this stage, it is of little or no use to reason with a baby who is irritated or hungry, since it is not the rational part of the brain that can tackle the problem. The only release is to meet their needs and comfort the baby when hungry, cold or sleepy. Once the child has turned one, the emotional part of the brain coexists with the reptilian, and parents must use different types of strategies to be able to communicate both with the child's most primitive instincts and their emotional need for love and security. At this level, limits, empathy and above all affection, are the most useful strategies for any parent. A little later, when the child is around three years old, the rational brain takes on a leading role in the child's life. They can now control their basic instincts and are guided by reason, intuition and will. However, they will still need a great deal of affection and understanding in order to gain control of their emotional brain.

When tired, sleepy and hungry (especially at the end of the day), the reptilian brain is still able to take control over their behaviour. In these cases, the crying child can barely find comfort in the words of the adult, and as with a baby their only requirement is that their most primary needs are met, in other words, to be fed or left to sleep. Below I have put together a table

Part of the brain	Experience of the child	Effective strategies
Reptilian brain	They are hungry, sleepy or in pain. They cry unconsolably.	Satisfy their needs. Soothe their anguish.
Emotional brain	They feel excited, frightened or frustrated. They are having a tantrum and want something.	Help the child to get what they want or to accept what they can't have. Empathise. Give them security and affection. Help them to think, to concentrate or to remember. Help them to connect with their emotional brain.
Rational brain	They remember relevant facts, they want to devise a plan to get something, they want to concentrate. They feel dissatisfied or worried.	Help them to think, to concentrate or to remember. Help them to connect with their emotional brain.

that might be useful in understanding how to deal with each level of brain processing.

An intelligent parent can establish a dialogue with each part of the child's brain at the moment in which that part takes control. The mother of a child who is disappointed because their teacher has not chosen them to be the class helper can talk to the child and help them to understand their desires and feelings. The dad of a child who is happy and eager to play, will lie down on the floor to play, and the mum of the child who is frustrated and angry because it is getting late will decide to swap dinner for a glass of milk to enable the child to have the rest they so need. Keeping these three levels of brain processing in mind can be very useful in helping the child calm down and move forward in all kinds of day-to-day situations. In the following chapters we will explore strategies to help you to connect with the different levels of brain processing, and more importantly, to teach your child to communicate with all parts of his or her brain.

5

Balance

A good head and a good heart are always a formidable combination.
(Nelson Mandela)

In my opinion, one of the fundamental pillars that every parent or educator must have in mind when educating their children is balance. Buddhists call this balance "middle way," and according to them, it is a way to achieve wisdom. In this book we are going to pay close attention to balance in the education of children. First, let's pause to look at the importance of supporting a balanced development between the emotional and the rational brain. Second, we are going to refer to balance as the ability to employ common sense when it comes to educating a child and making decisions regarding their care.

Emotional brain and rational brain

Most parents want two things for their children: for them to be happy and for them to be able to fend for themselves. In many cases, they put great effort into their academic education, convincing themselves that a brilliant mind will open doors for them to become a happy person. Work, love, friendships, success and a certain degree of comfort. However, the assumption that greater intellectual development promotes greater happiness is extremely misguided. In reality, the correlation between rational intelligence and emotional intelligence is zero. For those who are not familiar with statistics, I will explain the data: there is no relationship between the intellectual capacity and the emotional capacity of a person. This is a fact that you have most likely been able to verify for yourselves. The world is full of people with intellectual abilities to spare, but who do not have empathy, who suffer from chronic stress or who, despite having the greatest success, fail to find happiness. Similarly, you have surely met people without academic studies, with a modest intellectual development yet who, in spite of this, are warm, welcoming and full of common sense.

DOI: 10.4324/9781003360117-7

The reason that this discrepancy may exist is very simple. As we have already seen, emotional and rational intelligence are located in very different areas of the brain, and therefore are independent of one another. While the whole rational cortex tries to get the child to relate to the world through their intellectual abilities, the emotional brain is governed by the laws of emotions. If for the rational brain a better result is achieved through greater analysis of the situation, for the emotional brain the first impressions and the experience itself lead the decision-making process. It is not that there is a better or worse way of thinking; different circumstances require greater emotional or intellectual intelligence. Moreover, we know that people who achieve a good working balance between these two brains are not only the happiest, but are those with the greatest capacity to accomplish their goals. In this sense, a balanced education is one that pays as much attention to the intellectual brain as to the emotional one. Not just so that each one of them develops fully, but especially so that they know how to communicate with each other, so the child can grow into an adult who can live their emotions, feelings and thoughts in harmony.

Educate with common sense

With regard to education, possibly one of the most common mistakes among parents is to go to extremes. Interestingly, this attitude is relatively frequent among parents who read more and who are more informed about how they should educate their children. The extremes can occur in any direction, but the "fundamentalist" parent has fixed and precise ideas regarding the best way to educate their children and tends to place little value on other options and those who practise them. However, children grow up healthy and happy whether in an Inuit tribe, in the middle of the jungle or travelling with a herd of camels through the desert. The reality is that the cereal that we spoon into their bottles of milk does not need to be measured out by the millimetre; nothing will happen if moisturising lotion is not applied one evening; nor when the child becomes frustrated if the mom or dad decides to finish buttoning her/his own shirt before reaching down to pick up the child. Raising a child is much simpler and more instinctive than we are led to believe. Of course, carrying our baby, establishing limits, feeding them on demand or picking them up is positive for their development, but it is also important to do it in a relaxed way, in order to transmit a sense of calm. Helping them every time they cry is of little use if we are on edge or tense when we pick them up, if they were crying for a moment more than they should have been. Dealing with children calmly is a way to convey our confidence; and this can be just as important as the very act of attending to them when they need us.

There is much evidence to suggest that extremes are no better than taking a moderate course of action. As everyone knows, germs can cause infections and digestive disorders; therefore, many paediatricians recommend that bottles, dummies (or pacifiers) and teats are sterilised during the first months of life. In some cases, parents can become overly obsessed with creating a completely sterile world. However, according to a recent study in Sweden published by the prestigious journal *Pediatrics*, parents who clean their child's dummy by putting it into their mouths – without using water or anything else – are giving their children a greater diversity of bacteria in their digestive systems, which benefits the immune system. These children are less likely to suffer from asthma and skin eczema than other children whose dummies are always properly sterilised.

Another polarised belief is that setting few limits for the child is better, or at the other end of the scale, that many limits must be set. In the first instance, the child can grow up with an absence of rules. This can result in a lack of confidence, since they have not been able to internalise fundamental social rules. In the second instance, the child can grow up being too self-conscious and, as in the first example, lack confidence because they feel they are being monitored too much. There are likewise conflicting beliefs about how to deal with a baby's sleep. Some parents strenuously support co-sleeping and others believe the child should only sleep on their own. The latter group claim that teaching a child autonomy from a very young age is crucial, while the former group strongly uphold the necessity of physical contact to prevent the baby or the child experiencing distress or frustration. In many cases each believe that only their way is valid, but studies indicate that each formula has its benefits, as long as each is based on the premise that the baby will be attended to when it cries. The reality is that most parents choose neither one strategy nor the other, and usually combine different options in order to teach their children, little by little, to develop positive routines for sleeping in their own bedroom.

As the book goes on, I will guide you along a more moderate path that will allow you to feel comfortable raising your children, so they are influenced in developing a balanced mind, with the ability to think clearly, as well as to feel good about themselves and others.

Part II

Tools

6
Tools for supporting brain development

The big artists keep their eyes on nature and steal her tools.

(Thomas Eakins)

One of the most characteristic features of the human brain is its ability to design and use tools. Tools have accompanied us since our appearance as a species and have been one of the key aspects of our progress and evolution. Thanks to tools, the human being – which is relatively slow compared to other animals – was able to hunt and eat meat. The change in diet, from one based on fruits and leaves, to one rich in protein, allowed our body to devote less energy to digestion, and more of those extra calories to the incredible adventure of thinking. In the same way, protein intake allowed us to turn those thoughts into brain connections, making the brain grow at a phenomenal rate. While man developed its intelligence, the brain designed another tool that revolutionised its possibilities: language. This was the definitive tool for transmitting knowledge about the location of the herds of animals, sharing and designing hunting strategies, explaining how to locate sources of water without having to accompany the person, and contemplating the future as a group. The design of tools has continued to evolve, helping us to progress as a species. As a reader, you currently have a tool in your hands that allows you to discover other points of view and learn through the experience of another human being, which is being explained to you through these words.

As you can see, tools have been a constant throughout evolution, allowing us to progress, and making difficult things easy. In all jobs and professions, human beings use tools, whether it is a hammer and nail, a mop and bucket, gloves and a scalpel, a blackboard and chalk, or a screen and a keyboard. However, parents have few tools at their disposal in the work of educating their children. There are all kinds of tools for the protection, care and transport of babies, such as prams, car seats, highchairs, bottles, bibs, dummies, nappies and bags for carrying the bottles, dummies and nappies. But aside

DOI: 10.4324/9781003360117-9

from books and educational toys, parents do not have any obvious tools to make their difficult job easier.

In my experience, however, I've learned that there are five tools that can support every parent in the complicated task of educating their child. Psychologists, pedagogues and educators have been using these tools for centuries. Neuroscientists have spent decades studying why and how they work. I can assure you that, if used properly, they are fully able to contribute to a balanced brain development. Although it is not enough to simply have them at hand to be able to know how to use them. Acquiring the skills to use these tools requires time and practice, but everyone can use them well if they understand when and why to use them, and how to pay attention to when they get it right, and when they don't.

You are going to learn to use five tools that are especially useful in a child's education. They are not the only tools we have – play and affection are perhaps even more important – but they are tools which I feel are most in need of an instruction manual, as we often lose our way when trying to use them.

7

Patience and understanding

Peace cannot be kept by force. It can only be achieved by understanding.
Attributed to Albert Einstein

From the birth of a baby to approximately eighteen months of age, the relationship between the child and their parents is relatively simple. The child needs food, rest and a great deal of affection. This is something that most parents can understand perfectly. However, as the child begins to move about, say a few words, and express their wishes, parents and children enter a somewhat more complex stage as far as their relationship is concerned. The reason is very simple: parents have often heard that the faculty of speech is what makes a human being rational. Therefore, as soon as the child begins to speak just a little, we begin to attribute all the virtues of reason (logic, self-control, responsibility ...) to them, and we lose our temper at the child when they are not reasonable or do not act as a rational adult would.

However, the brain of a child of one, two, or three years old is a long way from the brain of an adult; they cannot do many of the things that parents think that they can do. This difference between what the child can do and what the parents believe the child can do often creates misunderstandings, upsets and anger, which can often be avoided if we learn what is going on in their brains. In order for parents to understand and therefore show patience and compassion on a daily basis, we are going to look at three common situations that they will be able to deal with in a different way once they understand what is happening inside their young child's brain.

The long journey home from the supermarket

At around two years of age, the child is already able to run around the house and the park. Their way of doing it is always the same: the child is put on

DOI: 10.4324/9781003360117-10

the ground by their parent to go off and explore the sandpit, the swing or the slide. After a small tour of the park, the child returns to the bench where the parent is waiting. The child then goes back to play in the park and will return to her with a pebble or a spade that he or she has found on their expedition. The scene is repeated again and again, and the child does not stop walking all afternoon.

Encouraged by seeing their child walking around, many parents decide that it is time to leave the pram or baby carrier at home and walk to the supermarket together. It may go well on the way there, but on the way back, the child may no longer want to walk and asks to be carried. In the eyes of many parents, the child is making little effort and is being petulant. After all, the child spent the whole afternoon running around the park the day before! As a result, the parent begins to spout angry and disparaging phrases, blaming the child, such as "Don't give me that!" or the classic "You can but you just don't want to."

If we could see what occurs inside the child's brain in these two situations, we would realise that different things happen. In the first case, in the park, the child walks around in circles, always having his or her mother to hand, and can explore freely. To do this, the child only needs to have a little balance and a desire to explore.

However, on the trip back from the supermarket, the child's brain has to do something very different. In this case, the child needs the same balance as before, but they also need to concentrate (so they won't lose sight of their mother), they need persistence (to keep going even if they are tired) and, the most difficult of all, unlike what happened in the park, the child now has to suppress the desire to explore so they can concentrate on following their parent without getting distracted. At a cerebral level it is a much more complex and tiring activity. This is why children are usually not able to make the return journey home from the supermarket, as the way there provided a large amount of exercise that left them feeling exhausted.

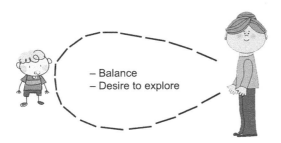

Balance – Desire to explore

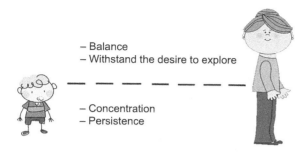

Balance – Withstand the desire to explore – Concentration – Persistence

As in many other instances, a little understanding from the parents can help solve a difficult situation in a simple way: carry the child, take the pram or baby carrier, or just stop to rest for a moment and then continue on your walk without any bad feeling.

Dinner time

Lunch or dinner time is usually a difficult moment for many families. The requirement of the child's brain to be cautious with food and taste things gradually clashes with the parents' desire for them to eat everything and finish everything on their plate. A child refusing their food causes the parents to employ two different strategies, which are as ineffective as they are unpleasant.

The first strategy is to force the child to eat the food that the child does not want to eat. The studies are clear in this regard; this strategy only generates more avoidance of these foods. It is normal for children to refuse to eat bitter or green foods, as most vegetables are, because at an instinctive level, the brain knows that many foods go darker and develop a bitter taste when they are rotten or in poor condition. It is also normal for parents to want their children to eat vegetables because they are very healthy for their development. However, forcing them is not the solution, because the child will end up becoming more averse to them. It is understandable; if you were forced to kiss a person you didn't like, after having to kiss them, you would find them even more disagreeable. You would even feel repulsed. Interestingly, the part of the brain that controls sexual desire in adults is close by, and it works in a similar way to the part that controls the appetite. When forced to eat food that they previously found disgusting, they are programmed to reject it with even more intensity, in some cases even for life.

You may remember a plate of spinach or Brussels sprouts that you were forced to eat when you were a child and that today you cannot even look at. The reason for this is because of what I have just explained.

The most effective strategy for preventing problems with food involves seven basic pillars of common sense, which are often absent in many households: (1) remove other more tempting, less healthy foods from the house (such as biscuits, crisps and sweets); (2) eat as a family so the child will imitate the adults when they eat vegetables; (3) always have vegetables on the table so that the child gets used to their appearance and smell; (4) let the child serve themselves, with a spoon or their hand, the amount which they deem appropriate (in my house, the rule is: "You can take a lot or a little, but you must always have at least a little bit on your plate"); (5) cut it up very small so that they can gradually get used to its flavour; (6) encourage them (never force them) to try a little – even if it is the size of a grain of rice – of new foods so that their brain gradually becomes used to the taste, and (7) possibly the most important one, have a laid back, relaxed atmosphere at the table, helping the child associate healthy food with love and a little fun.

The second strategy that many parents use at mealtimes is to force the child to finish their meal or to eat more than their appetite dictates. Studies are also clear about this: children know better than adults how much food they should eat. Rather than it being the amount that their parents say they must eat, the standard measure that children need on a nutritional level is usually the amount that the child puts on their own plate, divided by two. In other words, in many cases it is normal and healthy to leave half the food that was served because that amount is usually enough to provide all the calories their body needs. On one hand, obviously a three-year-old child who is 12 kilos in weight might not need the same amount of food as an adult weighing 80 kilos, who is also overweight. On the other hand, it is important to understand that a child's stomach is smaller and fills up and empties faster than an adult's. This is why the child's brain is quickly satiated and they demand food more frequently. It is hard to know where this custom comes from, in which many parents of our generation "force" the child to eat more. Perhaps the most likely explanation is that it comes from their great-grandmothers who educated their grandparents (our own parents) through difficult times; times in which they went hungry and when meat, fish and vegetables were not available every day. This was an era in which no one could guarantee that the child would have food to eat the following day. Fortunately, however, times have changed and in most households we don't have to worry about whether a child will have food to eat the next day. Therefore, we are able to rely on the child's own sensations to indicate how much they want to eat. It is the best way for the child to properly regulate their appetite from childhood to adulthood.

The perfect storm

One situation that all parents (and children) have to experience at some point, are tantrums. Tantrums are a universal phenomenon that happen to all (or nearly all) children, from all countries and cultures of the world. Despite this, most parents do not know how to react, and many tend to get annoyed with their children or are ashamed when they throw the classic tantrum. Some try everything to suppress it: shaming the child in front of the supermarket staff, threatening them, shouting, emotionally blackmailing them or walking away, leaving the child behind. They try these strategies because they think another adult may react. However, we know that with a two-year-old child there is nothing we can do.

Let's have a look at why tantrums occur. Around the age of two, the child begins to figure out their desires; the prefrontal cortex has already gathered enough persistence to persevere in achieving their goals. This is the age when tantrums begin. The child sees something they like, such as a doll in the shop window, they imagine playing with it and they can fight for it until they get it. Their parent realises that distracting them will no longer work, so they have no choice but to be direct and to give the child a clear "No." Although they may say it gently, when the child interprets that the refusal is immovable, immediately their brain will be engulfed in a perfect storm. All the emotional inertia, which gives them imagination and persistence, crashes head-on with their attempts to forget about the toy or calm down, and with the frustration caused by not being able to achieve either the first or second. All this results in a brutal clash of energies, a perfect storm that has a neurological explanation. Although the child has sufficient mental strength to persevere adamantly with what they want, they do not have the ability to calm their frustration because the neurons that help the child persevere with these actions or requests (which develop over two years of age) are different from those that slow down or inhibit behaviour or emotion. The latter, inhibitory neurons, do not develop until approximately four years of age. Soothing an emotion as intense as frustration is hard enough for adults, but for a two-year-old child whose inhibitory neurons are not yet developed, it is simply impossible, no matter how much we shame, threaten or scold them. The child will cry, scream and even kick, causing their brain to discharge all that accumulated energy into the "action" neurons, gradually helping them to calm down. However, many parents interpret these gestures as a "performance" or an attempt at manipulation and get even more angry, when in actual fact the child is not screaming, crying and kicking to get what they want – they are trying to release tension and calm down.

The parent's anger only makes the child's situation even more difficult, because their tasks build up: they must get rid of their excitement, they must calm their anger and, if this weren't enough, they must cope with two angry parents who are looking stern and saying horrible things to the child. The truth is that the child has a really bad time in these situations and the best way to help them is not by blackmailing them, becoming angry, or giving in to the request, but by following these steps, calmly and patiently:

1. Explain it to them. Normally explanations have no effect, but they will help a child develop their logical capabilities. In some cases, they do work, and when this happens, the relief for the child and for the parents is immense. Of course, explaining does not mean convincing or pressing. If your explanations do not satisfy them at the first or second attempt, move on to the next point.
2. Give them time. If the tantrum is already under way, the only certainty we have is that it will sooner or later pass. It is important to give the child enough time for the brain to discharge the energy that has built up. Don't rush it.
3. Don't move away. A child cannot survive without their parents, so moving away from them with threats like "Mummy is going home now," will only scare the child and the next time they will remember your reaction, become more distressed and the tantrum will be more serious.
4. Use empathy when you see the child has calmed down enough to listen. You can use simple phrases like "You wanted to stay and play a little longer didn't you?" As we will see later on, helping the child feel understood will make them calm down.
5. Offer to hold them when they ask for it, or when they have calmed down. Don't insist, and don't force them to, but if they ask for it or allow you to pick them up, remember that there is nothing wrong with helping the child to overcome their tantrum with a hug, or carrying them for a little while in your arms.

Instead of shouting, bribing them, shaming them or walking away, try:

1. Explaining your reasons.
2. Staying close to them.
3. Giving them time to get rid of all the built-up energy.
4. Empathise and make them know that you understand.
5. Hold out your arms when they ask for it, or when they are calmer.

In some cases, parents ask me if we should give in to tantrums. I always tell them that in general, no. If the child is given what they want during the course of a tantrum, they learn to become enraged in a deliberate way, in order to get what they want. However, it is fair to say that there are times when parents are wrong. I would not describe a two-year-old child who is crying because they are hungry fifteen minutes before a meal as having a tantrum.

Nor would I say that a child crying on a walk and asking to be carried is a tantrum. It is possible, as we have just seen, that the child is genuinely tired, and they don't want to be indulged; they actually need to be carried. Sometimes it is difficult to know when something is a whim or a desire and when it is a need. A good way to find out is to ask yourself if it responds to the child's four basic needs: (1) hunger, for example, they ask for a piece of bread; (2) sleep or tiredness, they want to go to sleep or can't walk anymore; (3) cold or hot, they want a blanket, and (4) protection and security, they ask for a hug. In these cases, it is usually sensible to answer to the child's need, and it is always better to realise it as soon as possible, before the child begins to lose control.

As you can see, tantrums are a natural and positive behaviour for children between the ages of two and four or five, at which time their brain can calm frustrations more efficiently. They indicate that their brain is developing correctly and that they have more imagination, capacity for desire and persistence than a one-year-old child. As with the walk to the supermarket or dinner time, being understanding and patient will help you solve conflicts more quickly and stay with your child when they need you most.

Remember

Children do not think or have the same mental abilities as adults and that is why we cannot assess their behaviour using the same techniques. While it is true that the job of parents and educators is to help them develop these skills, this is a process that happens very gently, and is why they need great understanding and patience on our part. These two skills will help us give them the time they need to develop at the pace that their brain sets, and furthermore without damaging the relationship between you.

8

Empathy

Could a greater miracle take place than for us to look through each other's eyes?

(Henry David Thoreau)

If I had to choose the most important skill for educating and helping children in their development, I would choose empathy. There are more and more studies which show that in the emotional development of the child, the most important thing is to feel understood.

The brain is basically a huge data processor. When you see a phone and are able to touch or listen to it, your brain perceives that the phone is real. When you smell a grilled steak and then taste it, your brain knows it's real. In the same way, when the baby latches on to their mother's breast, it knows two things: (1) that their mother is real and (2) that their hunger was also real, because the hunger disappeared after eating. Physical objects from the outside world are easy to "process" for a child, because they only have to stretch out their arm to be able to touch them, smell them or listen to how they sound when they shake them. However, feelings and emotions are much harder to verify because there is no way to reach out for them. The only way for a child to know that their emotions and feelings are real is to have an adult next to them who responds harmoniously to those needs, emotions and feelings.

This simple idea has a great impact on the emotional development of a child. According to the most recent studies, responding in a consistent manner (letting the child know that we understand and care for their needs) is the most important factor for the child to be able to develop a secure attachment. Secure attachment can be described as the level of confidence that the child feels towards the world, the security that they will have the resources and skills to cope on their own, and that someone will take care of them if they can't. In other words, it is the child's emotional confidence.

We know that when we take care of a hungry baby, we are strengthening their confidence because they feel cared for. When a one-year-old child is

DOI: 10.4324/9781003360117-11

scared and we take them in our arms, the child also strengthens their confidence, learning that their parents will help and they are confirming that the child's fear was real. As the child grows older, it is not so easy to respond to their needs because they are no longer primitive (hunger, fear, sleep) and they become more emotional and complex to understand. The three-year-old girl for example, who feels out of sorts after her baby brother is born, can feel jealous and come out with phrases that are hard to listen to for parents, such as "I hate my little brother." In this case, many parents can become angry or try to make the little girl reconsider what she has said. Although in truth, she is very scared and her brain, her data processor, needs someone to return the same information and to conform to her reality. In this example, the most appropriate answer would be something like this:

–I hate my little brother.
–I know, you don't like it that mummy is with him all the time.
–No, i don't ... (she is a little less grumpy).
–You're scared that mummy isn't paying you any attention.
–Yes (she relaxes).
–Well, i think we should leave the little baby asleep with daddy, and
    mummy can take you to the park on your own.
–Yessss! (She is now much happier).

As you can see in this example, responding with empathy to the child's feelings not only makes her understand that her feelings are real, but it also helps her to calm down. In this chapter, you will learn how to use empathy to understand your child and respond to them when they express their feelings. In this way, your child can understand themselves and therefore gain emotional intelligence, and you can help them to calm down when they feel out of sorts.

However, before we continue, I would like to clarify what empathy is.

What is empathy?

Empathy – from the Greek *em*, "in" and *pathos*, "suffering, feeling" – is a word used by psychologists to describe the ability to put oneself in another person's shoes. Unlike "sympathy", in which two people agree, there is no shared feeling in "empathy", although there is understanding. Let's give a very simple example. If you and your son love chocolate, when you see him getting really excited over chocolate bar that he has been offered, you will feel sympathy for his feelings. You would get excited too. If, on the other hand, your child loves sweets and you do not, when you see him jumping around over a bag of sweets you can feel empathy. You would not be jumping around, but knowing your son, you understand him and feel happy for him.

Sympathy   **Empathy**

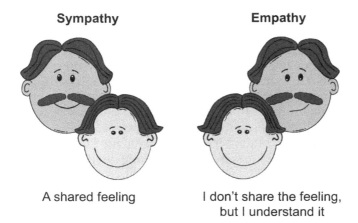

A shared feeling   I don't share the feeling,
                          but I understand it

Listening to a child with empathy will help them to understand and connect their emotions with their thoughts. It is, in short, a door to self-understanding and acceptance of oneself that we can use with the child from the moment they are born, covering them when they are cold, feeding them when they are hungry or helping them to relax and sleep when we think they are tired. As they grow older, parents continue to accompany the child on this journey of discovery and acceptance by listening to their anger, worries, dreams and fears. All those little conversations that parents have with their children who are sulking, sad or excited on the way home from school or in the corner of the kitchen, and then repeated many times throughout our lives, contribute greatly to giving them the ability to understand and trust. So do not hesitate: when your children need you, listen to them, because it is possibly the most important thing we can do as parents. You will notice that they calm down more quickly, they overcome their fears and anxieties and their confidence and your relationship grows.

Why empathy works

As you will remember, in a child's – and an adult's – brain, there are two universes: the emotional brain and the rational brain. Both worlds tend to function independently, and when we experience a very intense emotion it is almost impossible to contain it. It is like a horse that has bolted, and neither the teacher nor the parent, never mind the child, is able to calm them down. The reason why empathy is such a powerful tool is because when the person hears an empathetic response, a wonderful effect occurs in their brain. The rational brain and the emotional brain tune in, and this has a calming effect on the emotional brain. This happens because empathic responses activate one of the areas that act as a bridge between both worlds. An area that is

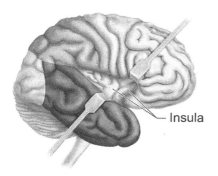

Insular cortex
• Taste and smell
• Interprets body language
• Identifies emotions
• Experiences emotions
  – Love
  – Disgust
  – Hate
  – Sadness

Insula

located in a strategic enclave between the emotional and the rational brain, hidden in a deep fold that can only be accessed by separating the temporal, parietal and frontal lobes. We know this isolated region between the two worlds as "insula."

When a region of the emotional brain is over-excited due to frustration, sadness or any other intense emotion, the child is not be able to contain their mood. This is when the tantrums occur – situations in which the child closes in on themselves and is not able to do what they are told – or comments are made which the parents find hard to deal with. Literally, the child is outside themselves, outside their rational part. To help them calm down, and to see reason, the best strategy is a hug and an empathic reflection of the situation to defuse the intensity of the emotion. A spoken word that will form a bridge between the two worlds, allowing the child's rational brain to help soothe their emotions, or at least give them the ability to listen to what their parents are saying.

Educate with empathy

The main difficulty in using empathy as a tool for brain development is that most parents find it hard to manage and understand their own emotions. As we said before, most adults often feel overwhelmed, or at least bewildered, by our own emotions. We can feel angry, sad or frustrated without apparent reason, and we don't understand how we are really feeling or what got us into that mood in the first place. Only some people can accurately understand their feelings, their emotions and their needs and act wisely on them, usually as a result of therapy, which teaches them self-awareness and personal growth. Without a doubt, these people have a clear advantage when dealing with the emotional education of their children, because they have a deeper knowledge of themselves and the world of emotions. For many other adults, teaching emotions can be as difficult as an illiterate teacher trying to teach his or her students to read. If you really want to grow your own knowledge – and thus help your children – I recommend beginning therapy in personal growth. For those who are not quite there – and for everyone else – a good exercise is to reconnect with your dictionary of emotions.

Most adults are equipped with the emotional vocabulary that would be found in a book such as *Learn English in Three Weeks*. The most familiar way for adults to describe their feelings is "good" and "bad"; which are not even feelings. Some are able to identify, in a moment of introspection and openness to the world, four other feelings: "happy", "sad", "angry" and "annoyed" – including all the offensive varieties of the latter. In reality, we all know roughly a hundred words to express emotions and feelings, but we do not use them in our daily lives. This is because society tells us that speaking about our emotions in public is not appropriate, and also because it is difficult for us to identify a specific word for a feeling that we cannot clearly identify. Fortunately, times are changing and nowadays we know that being in touch with our emotions brings many advantages; the main one being that of increasing our emotional intelligence.

To help students wanting to improve their empathy and understand how empathy works, I usually ask them to imagine that the world of emotions is like a large radio. In that radio we have different frequencies, or basic emotions, and each of those frequencies can be heard at a higher or lower volume. Grief and sadness are on the same emotional frequency, but grief has a lower volume. Joy and euphoria are also on the same frequency, and in this case, euphoria is louder. When giving an effective empathic response, it is very important to be on the same frequency as the emotion experienced by the person but also to tune in to its volume. Imagine you are a twenty-year-old who goes to a party on a Saturday night and the host spends all evening playing Viennese waltzes. This type of music is not likely to be in tune with the mood of the guests, and some will leave the party feeling disappointed. The result would be similar if the music genre was more popular, for example rock music, but the volume was so low that it could barely be heard over people talking. In the same way, a couple of teenagers wanting a romantic moment in the back of the car, will choose a chilled-out radio station on a low volume. A jukebox ballad played at full blast will not contribute to an intimate setting, nor will some hard rock played at a low volume. Therefore, if you want to empathise with your child, it is important that you know how to tune in to their emotions. When it comes to responding with empathy to your child and connecting with them, getting the emotional frequency right is just as important as the intensity. If your son cries unconsolably because he has just lost his sticker collection, you will not tune in to his emotions if you tell him off for losing them. This is not empathy. Nor will he respond well if you tell him that he is angry, because his feelings are more in tune with sadness. The best way to get the child to open up and calm down is to acknowledge that he must be "really really sad" or "heartbroken" and offer him a big hug that subdues his feeling of disconsolation. In the same way, if Molly has just adopted a snail as her new pet and is showing it to the whole family with a delighted face, she may not connect with a comment such as: "You are happy", as the intensity is short-lived. It would be much better for the parent to say enthusiastically: "Molly, you are really excited about your new pet, aren't you?". This comment is more likely to help her feel understood, so she can share all the plans she has for her new friend with her parent, like the house they will build for it, or what they will feed it. On the following page there are two tables with some key emotions, which are arranged by frequency and intensity.

These tables only include around fifty feelings and emotions. The repertoire of human emotions is much larger and you will be able to identify nuances in the expressions of your children. However, these fifty emotions form a repertoire that is wide enough to be able to talk with your children about any subject, and calm them down in almost any situation, helping them to understand their own feelings. You will notice that I have not classified emotions as "positive" and "negative", as is usually the case. The reason for this is very simple. All emotions are positive in themselves; therefore it is important to recognise and give them their space within the child's world. We should not stigmatise any feeling, as all of them are important. Anger

Pleasant emotions

			Frequencies		
	Placidity	Joy	Love	Motivation	Satisfaction
-	At ease	Happy	Charmed	Lively	Proud
	Comfortable	Cheerful	Friendly	Motivated	Acknowledged
	Tranquil	Excited	Affectionate	Emotional	Satisfied
	Relaxed	Glad	Like	Excited	Happy
		Euphoric	Love	Dedicated	
+			Infatuated	Enthusiastic	
Intensity					

Unpleasant emotions

			Frequencies			
	Anger	Anxiety	Fear	Frustration	Sadness	Tiredness
+	Throwing a	Anxious	Frightened	Furious	Inconsolable	Exhausted
	tantrum	Flustered	Scared	Frustrated	Hurt	Fed up
	Angry	Restless	Overwhelmed	Aggravated	Sad	Bored
	Irritated		Embarrassed		Disappointed	Tired
	Annoyed		Worried		Saddened	
-	Upset		Nervous		Feeling sorry	
Intensity						

can help us fight for our life in a given situation; frustration helps us do better the next time; and sadness helps us to perceive the beauty of things and to value our needs, as well as to understand the feelings of others.

Let's practise

Mary is inconsolable. She wanted to go to the park, but it has started to rain. She has been crying for five minutes and she is getting louder and louder.

Instead of saying: "Mary, calm down. Don't worry ...
another day we'll go to the park".

Try: "I know, it's so annoying isn't it? You were really looking forward to going to the park, weren't you?".

Alexander is throwing a tantrum. You are leaving the supermarket and he wants you to buy him a lollipop.

Instead of saying: "Alexander. Stop crying. I am not buying you a lollipop".

Try: "I understand, you are really angry because you want mummy to buy you a lollipop".

Stephanie arrives home after school feeling sad, although she can't explain why.

Instead of saying: "Come on Stephanie, let's cheer ourselves up.
Shall we play princesses?"

Try: "You're a little bit sad, aren't you?" "Yes, a little", "I know, I can see it in your face that something's the matter".

Clearly, giving words of empathy to a boy having a tantrum in a supermarket is not going to calm him down immediately, but you must persevere. It is advisable to share a few empathic words with the child, while you try to pacify him and encourage him to be calm. With the initial words of empathy, you can get his attention, but it will take four or five comments, or all those that are necessary to sufficiently reduce the child's level of discomfort.

Empathy is not only reflected through words. An understanding look, a caress, a kiss or a hug can help them understand much more than words can. Don't be afraid to join your child in feeling their emotions through a physical display of affection. Taking them in your arms and giving them a kiss or a big hug will help them to feel understood and to calm down.

One last piece of advice: to be able to listen to a child with empathy, it is important to detach ourselves from our adult world, ignoring our dogmas and prejudices. Put yourself in the child's shoes, enter your child's mind and consider how they feel. How would you feel if you were in their position? Let's use an example. Try to imagine how you would feel if the person you loved most in the whole world – your husband or wife – was having an affair with someone like you, but younger and sweeter. Surely this is the same feeling as the child who finds out that his or her mother – the person they love most in the world – will be spending more time with their newborn brother than with them. Don't you think you would hate him a little bit too?

Remember

Empathy is a very valuable tool for providing the child with security and growing their self-esteem. All emotions are important and valuable. Listening to the child with empathy will help them identify their feelings and improve their emotional intelligence. Empathy is also a useful tool in helping the child to cope with whatever comes their way, to calm themselves down in situations where they feel overwhelmed by anguish, anger or frustration. An empathic response can help subdue intense emotions when the child cannot do it themselves.

9

Reinforcing rules and positive behaviour

Never discourage anyone who continually makes progress, no matter how slow.

Plato

In the last two chapters we have seen how patience, understanding and empathy are essential for educating our children, for them to have high self-esteem. However, the job of educating does not end here. All parents understand the child's desire to play and experience things, although they don't usually enjoy when their children try to dangle off the curtain rails. Furthermore, even though they agree that children must learn on their own in order to form relationships, they often feel a need to intervene if their child pulls another child's hair or tries to steal their toy. It is also normal for parents to want to encourage their children to finish the trip to the supermarket without being carried because they want to help them become a little more resilient each day. Or simply because they want the child to understand that mummy and daddy also get tired when they have to carry them. Being understanding is very important, but so is helping the child to overcome obstacles and understand the needs of others, as well as to know common societal rules. If the former allows the child to develop self-esteem, the latter allows the child to develop confidence. Both are essential in helping the child to feel good.

In the following chapters we will focus on how you can help the child to understand and respect the rules that you feel are important for their education and which are based on your own values and convictions. We know that each culture and each household has different rules. I like to see my children running around barefoot, but in other houses slippers must be worn. You could say that there are as many rules as there are parents, but it is always the same part of the brain that is responsible for adapting these rules so that the child can satisfy his or her needs while following the rules set by society and by the family with whom they live. In order to instill these rules

DOI: 10.4324/9781003360117-12

into the child's brain with any success while allowing them to achieve their own goals and independence, two conditions have to be met. First, the rules should be set by imposing limits and enforcing them. Second, it is important to indicate to the child what behaviour is appropriate and to help their brain store that in a positive way.

Later we will talk about how these limits can be set and enforced. In this chapter I am going to teach you how you can help your child to learn and store some positive rules and behaviour for their development, giving you a few strategies that are both simple and effective.

Showing positive models of conduct

Children develop a considerable part of their intellectual and emotional abilities through observation and imitation. If you have more than one child, you will be able to recall countless situations in which the younger child imitated the elder. In the same way, both will imitate you, in the good and the bad. This type of imitation is a very primary way of learning and of brain development. Young zebras run away from lions simply because all the other zebras do. In exactly the same way, children who have seen their mother scream in terror at a spider, may develop a fear of spiders. The brain has a circuit of neurons whose main purpose is to learn through observation. Every time a baby observes how their father says their name, this circuit, known as "mirror neurons", begins to picture the baby's own lips and tongue moving in the same way. When a child sees their mother being respectful and dealing with her problems calmly, or conversely, losing her temper and treating another person with contempt, the child's brain learns to picture themselves acting in the same way. Like a mirror that reflects what it sees, mirror neurons silently rehearse many of your own behaviours, programming the child's brain as a preparation, so that they can repeat them in similar situations.

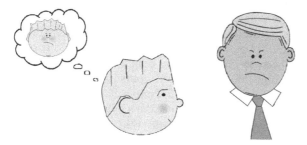

When the child sees his father frustrated with anger,
the child's brain allows him to imagine himself
with the same anger.

So, the first lesson in promoting proper behaviour is for you to provide a good model for your child to imitate. It is of little use if we try as hard as we can for our son to acquire positive thinking if all he hears from his parent are pessimistic comments. It is almost impossible to teach respect for others if the child hears his or her parents criticising each other and other people. Regarding development, there is one area in which good models of conduct have proven crucial for the child's learning; and that is managing anger and frustration. There are so many studies showing that children learn to become angry and manage their anger based on what they see from their parents, that I find it impossible to pick just one. However, to summarise, I can tell you that boys tend to replicate the behaviour and expressions of their father to a greater degree, and girls, those of their mother. The effect we have on our children is very powerful. Making a dismissive comment to a child just once, such as: "You have no idea", is enough for them to begin to treat their younger siblings or classmates with disdain. Angrily telling off a three-year-old just once is enough for them to begin to show anger at school, shouting at their classmates. In fact, studies indicate that parents who educate their children with a heavy hand (shouting at them, punishing them harshly or spanking them) are very likely to be expelled from school at some point, get into fights, or have unwanted pregnancies during their adolescence. It is understandable; their parents taught them by example to lose control in countless situations.

But I don't want to focus on the negatives. Modelling (teaching our children through example) is, above all, an opportunity to show your children positive skills. If you want your child to have the strength to defend themselves against abuse, do not let yourself be pushed around time and again by your boss, your sibling, or your partner. If it is important for you that your child is honest, be honest with them and with other people. If it is important that they eat fish, serve yourself a big plate of roast salmon, and if it is important that they enjoy life and are happy, start by enjoying both the little and big moments that life hands you. In this sense, I encourage you to take advantage of being a parent as an opportunity to be the best version of yourself. Every father, every mother and every teacher has a responsibility to educate through example, and you can use that opportunity to your own gain. Show your child how the best version of you behaves, show them how you stand up for your rights, how you achieve your goals in your career, social relationships or in your search for happiness. I can assure you that your child's brain will absorb this teaching by example like a sponge.

Being the best version of yourself does not imply that you should try to make others think you are perfect, because neither you nor anyone else is. Don't be afraid to show yourself as you are. My children have seen me laugh, cry, get angry, ask for forgiveness, make mistakes, and also get things right. I try not to hide anything, and I show myself as I am. However, I also try to tap into my entire repertoire of human behaviours in the child's favour. When I feel sad, I show them that it is good to express your emotions and ask for help. When I get angry, I try to do it in an appropriate way, showing them that their father, like everyone else, has the right to be angry. Then, when I am happy or experience positive emotions, I transmit it to them. In areas such as health, I have tried to improve myself to become a good example for them. Two weeks after my first child was born, I stopped smoking. I was a heavy smoker and nobody around me thought I would be able to quit. However, by reflecting on the influence that my own image will have on my child, I decided that I didn't want him to have the example of a father who was a smoker engrained in his mind. I meditated one day, and gave up suddenly, without patches or medication. I was motivated solely by the desire to be a good example for my children. I recognise that it is not always this easy but certainly trying is always better than nothing.

> "Your child will look at you as a model person. Show them how the best version of yourself behaves."

Reinforcing positive behaviour

More and more I hear from parents expressing their concern about reinforcing behaviour after reading a book about the Montessori method, or after talking to a friend who is not trained in psychology or neurology. There is a common conception that reinforcing children's positive behaviours can make them dependent on these reinforcements (the child only does what they are told is right) or narcissistic (the child thinks they do everything well). Indeed, there are studies that show that if we reinforce behaviour indiscriminately, the child may end up believing that they are some sort of God, or if we reinforce every little thing they do well, he may end up being too dependent on the appraisal of others. As you can imagine, in this topic, as in many others, extremes are often harmful, and it is obvious that constantly reinforcing a child's behaviour can be negative for their self-esteem. However, all studies indicate that reinforcements given at the right time and at the appropriate frequency are fundamental to their education. I assure you, that if you know when and how you should reinforce certain behaviours, you will have won 90 per cent of the education battle, and raising your children will be infinitely more satisfying for both of you, because parents need children to acquire behavioural habits gradually and children usually feel more secure if they understand and know to play according to the rules.

To reinforce means to strengthen a behaviour and, far from being a "conduct-based" distortion of educating a child, it is an entirely natural tendency. The truth is that you cannot educate without reinforcing, because reinforcement is something as natural as smiling at a child who shows you something with pride, or showing your satisfaction when they learn a new skill. Reinforcements are numerous; from a material reward, like a toy, to a smile. However, keep in mind that studies have shown time and again that material rewards are very ineffective as a reinforcement (and even counterproductive).

Rather, the most effective reinforcements are the simple gestures. The most interesting thing about reinforcements, is not what you do or what the child does, but what happens in their brain when they are rewarded. Each time the child feels reinforced, special neurons, located in the area of the brain that controls motivation, secrete a substance known as dopamine. Dopamine allows the child's brain to associate behaviour with a feeling of satisfaction or reward. To put it in the simplest way possible, we can say that satisfaction produces dopamine, and dopamine allows two ideas, two neurons, to join together. I am going to give a very clear example so that you understand it perfectly. If one day, driven by curiosity, your little boy opens a box kept in the kitchen cupboard, and discovers that it is full of chocolate biscuits, his brain will immediately experience great satisfaction. That satisfaction will allow him to associate this particular act – and being curious in general – with *a feeling of satisfaction*. Very quickly, the neurons associated with hunger will connect with those that represent the box of biscuits.

When I open the box of biscuits,
I satisfy my hunger and I feel good.

This simple thing that you have just understood is the basic mechanism of learning. Thanks to the reward he earned, the child has learnt that this box contains lots of chocolate biscuits that satisfy his need for sugar. This is a very powerful idea, because every parent, when trying to educate their child, ultimately wants the child to learn, to make connections in their brain that allow them to be autonomous, to achieve their goals and to be happy. The child will learn habits, ways of thinking, principles, values and knowledge from you. If you manage to associate the actions that you think are beneficial to them with the reward of feeling satisfied or acknowledged, you will help motivate their behaviour in an appropriate manner.

The ways to apply this very basic principle are almost infinite: from helping your child to stop using nappies, encouraging an enjoyment of reading, or in taking care of basic tasks such as getting dressed and eating. When you learn to reinforce your child properly, you will see how moments of anger and frustration are fewer, because their brain learns what it is before it happens, and that it is not always appropriate. Let's look further at this.

How to reinforce

There are many ways to reinforce; some are effective, others ineffective and others are even counterproductive. When you reward your child, you must do so in a way that is *proportionate*. It makes no sense to the child's brain if, when turning off the television after being asked to do so, he is rewarded with a Star Wars doll, and then getting into the bath without being told to only warrants a "well done". In the same way, we know that the most effective rewards are those that are *in tune* with their behaviour. Therefore, if the child gets into the bath when you ask him to, the best reinforcement would be to fill the bath with bubbles or to have a bath with him, and if he has turned off the television the best reinforcement would be to do something that can be done with the television off, such as having a playfight with the cushions.

The types of reinforcement or reward we choose are also very important, because there are some that are ineffective or even counterproductive, and others that are more satisfying for the child, and therefore more effective. In general, although it may seem otherwise, material reinforcements are less rewarding, and consequently less effective than emotional reinforcements. In this sense, I assure you that the Star Wars doll is less effective than the playfight, even if it doesn't seem so. This is for two reasons. First, the brain more easily associates groups of neurons that are closer together. In other words, it associates more socially appropriate behaviour, the television being off, with a social activity, playfighting, rather than with a material object, the Star Wars doll.

Second, because a game with an adult creates a different emotional reaction than that of the doll. Playing with an adult is more effective in activating the neurons that secrete dopamine, and therefore the reinforcement of appropriate behaviour is stronger. As we can see in the above representation, in the second case, the amount of connections – the association that will be created between neurons – is greater than in the first.

Material reward
When I obey →
I get something I want.

Emotional or social reinforcement
When I obey →
I feel satisfied.

The danger of using material rewards goes beyond their ineffectiveness. Every time you give your child a reinforcement, you are sending them a message. If you play with the child or thank them when they do what they are asked, or help you, the child will understand that by cooperating, they are unified with other people, and this is an important value. If, on the other hand, you give the child a toy when they do something, they will understand that possessing things is valuable in life. Therefore, when they are older, they will surely need to have many possessions in order to feel satisfied or rewarded. If you think there is any possibility that your son or daughter will not grow up to be a millionaire, and that they won't always be able to buy that treat that makes them feel special or important, it is possible that you are programming your child to feel worthless and unhappy. Even if you are certain that your child will live in the lap of luxury when they are older, using material rewards is still a bad strategy; the child will be slower to learn and will not fully understand the value of love or helping one another. I am convinced that the fewer material rewards, the better.

Something similar occurs with food. If you teach your child that every time they behave well they will be given a treat, a sweet, or a bag of crisps, you will be doing them a great disservice. Sweets and fatty foods can cause a spike in sugar that is very pleasurable for the child's brain. With regard to brain chemistry, it is difficult to compete with the sugar rush of a chocolate bar, and possibly when they grow up and want to feel satisfied, their brain will demand sweets or some other product to satisfy the sugar dependence that we have created. If you do not want your child to use food as a way of feeling good about themselves, I recommend that you don't use it as a reward either. In some cases, it can be reinforced with activities that involve having something sweet. If, for example, during the summer the child is behaving well, we can reward them with a trip to the ice cream shop, an activity in which a walk outside with a parent is just as important as the ice cream.

However, as a general rule I recommend that you reinforce your child with a social reward. Such as thanking them, congratulating them, granting them a small privilege, such as helping you to take out the rubbish, or giving them your time and sitting on the floor to play their favourite game. Below you can see a list of rewards, ordered according to their effectiveness and ineffectiveness.

Effective rewards	Rewards that are less effective
• Spend time playing with what the child wants to play with.	• Toys and other material rewards
• Give them a responsibility (carrying the keys).	• Food.
• Grant them a privilege (choosing what's for dinner).	• Tell them that they have done it well but can do it better.
• Tell them they have done it well.	• Congratulate them in front of others, to the point that they become embarrassed
• Congratulate them.	
• Thank them.	

It is very important that you take into account the likes and preferences of your child when selecting the rewards. Some children like to help their parents cook and others prefer to help wash the car. For some children, the best reinforcement would be to paint with their parent and for others to read a nice story together.

Either way, try to remember that the reward should not be the driving force of the child, rather, a pleasant consequence that helps to repeat positive behaviour, so it can come about spontaneously. It is of little use for the child to clear the dishes in exchange for sitting down to paint with mum; they will not learn the importance of fulfilling their responsibility, but merely how useful it is to do so. In this sense, it is important to keep in mind that reinforcements should be given after the child has done something valuable ("You have cleared the table so well that we are going to read two stories tonight") and that it should not be offered as an exchange for something else ("If you clear the table well, we will read two stories"). Although it may seem a subtle difference, for the child's brain it is of huge importance, because they are learning two different things. In the first case, the child grows in confidence and satisfaction. In the second case, the child will feel that their parents do not trust them and that they are more like a donkey who needs a carrot to behave properly.

**"You have cleared
the table so well!
Let's read two stories!"**

When I help with a
task, I feel good.

**"If you clear
the table well,
we can read two stories."**

When there is a reward,
I fulfil the task.

When to reinforce

1. When it is necessary. The first thing you should know is that reinforcement is something natural that occurs in life. When a child investigates and finds something interesting, they experience satisfaction; when a boy speaks to his brother who is a few months old, and he looks back at him, he feels satisfaction, and when the baby reciprocates, he also experiences the pleasure of connecting with another human being. It is not necessary for us to acknowledge and reward each thing our child does, because words of recognition can lose value if they are repeated too much. It is better to reward when we see progress, a new and positive attitude – such as effort or concentration – when the child corrects a mistake or when they want to share their joy.

2. Immediately. We know that the sooner the reward comes after the behaviour, the more effective the reward is. The brain acts in fractions of a

second, so associating one behaviour with another, such as that of tidy-ing away their toys and a pleasant sensation, or appreciative words from their mum, means that the two experiences must be in close succession.

3. Spaced out. Sometimes it is not easy to give the reward immediately, because some challenges and tasks require large rewards. Suppose you set a goal for your oldest child to put her dirty clothes in the basket every day for a week. This can be a difficult goal for a young child to maintain, but we can help her to feel satisfied by drawing a tick on the blackboard, or by putting a smiley face on a piece of paper next to the laundry basket every time she does it right. In this way, we are not only allowing the child to feel rewarded by way of recognition each time she does it well, but we are helping her to postpone the final reward by di-viding it into small, more achievable pleasures. This is a genuinely dif-ficult skill for the brain, which helps to distinguish between those who are capable of achieving their goals, and those who are not. Therefore, helping to divide long-term goals into small pleasures is a strategy that will help them.

4. When the child does it better. Possibly the most frequent mistake I have seen in the education of children, is that of parents who do not know how to reward change. Frequently, parents may encounter situations that they do not like. A child who hits his brother, or who bites his classmates, or simply a child who does not want to get dressed when we ask them to. At this point I am going to give you a piece of advice that is worth your child's weight in gold: do not wait for their behaviour to become the appropriate sort. Reward the child when they do things a little better or a little less badly than the day before.

For fifteen years I have been working with patients with severe and very severe behavioural problems, and I can assure you that in every case, the key to getting them to adopt good behaviour involves evaluating and focusing on small improvements. It would certainly be wonderful if some-one was able to change overnight; if we could say to a two-year-old boy, "Jamie, I want you to stop biting people", and he immediately changed his way of behaving. However, we know that the brain does not work like that. The brain changes little by little, based on repetition and successive approximations. I like to explain that provoking change in a child's brain is like creating a new path through a field of grass. In order for the child to get used to going along a new path, they must first step outside of the old one.

Secondly, they must continue walking along in the direction that we show them. Thirdly, they have to walk along that route many times – over days and weeks – so that the grass is well trod, and a dirt path begins to form. And, finally, you must trust that the grass will grow over the old path where we don't want to go back to. In this sense, there is no better way to motivate a child's behaviour than to reinforce it when they set foot on the path we want them to follow.

Trick-reinforcement

Trick-reinforcements are those treats, rewards or reinforcements that hide another sentiment and that are therefore counterproductive.

1. Reinforcements that show dissatisfaction. When we use a positive situation to show dissatisfaction or to ask for a little more, instead of feeling the satisfaction that would serve as reinforcement, the child's brain experiences frustration. For example, if Angela's mother says: "You have put everything away, but I have had to ask you three times", the girl will feel that her mother disapproves of her behaviour and will learn that it is not worth the effort.
2. Reinforcements that express resentment or awaken guilt. When your child behaves properly when getting dressed, you make a comment like: "That's great Richard, you've done well getting dressed today, unlike other days", he will immediately feel the weight of the criticism and the reinforcement will have lost its purpose.
3. Reinforcements that express obligation. When we say to a child: "Well done, Alice, I hope that you'll do it like that from now on", her brain will immediately detect that the comment is expressing a demand rather than a reward. Instead of satisfaction, her brain will experience frustration.

The following is a representation of what happens in the child's brain when faced with a trick-reinforcement.

When I make an effort or behave well
→ I feel sad or frustrated.

As you can see, the immediate effect on the child is that of sadness or frustration. In the short term, the reinforcement will be ineffective, because the child's brain did not experience any satisfaction, and it may take time for them to behave well again. The long-term effect of repeating this trick-reinforcement is that the child will experience an emotional remoteness from their parent, since the dissatisfaction caused by these poisoned arrows will cause them to distance themselves emotionally from their parents.

Instead of saying...	**Try saying...**

"You have done it really well but you could do better."	"You've done it so well."
"Well done, you've got dressed by yourself, unlike other days."	"You've got dressed on your own! Go Richard!"
"Alice, you have done it very well, I hope you'll always do it like that."	"Alice, you're a champion."

Remember

One of the most important characteristics of parents who are successful in their job as educators is that they use reinforcements to strengthen or motivate positive behaviour. Don't reinforce the child at all times; in most cases their own satisfaction is the best reinforcement. The best time to reinforce behaviour is when you are teaching them a new skill, or when they have made progress with a specific behaviour. Most importantly, reinforce your child with recognition, time and love, and set aside material rewards and food.

10

Alternatives to punishment

Help others achieve their dreams and you will achieve yours.

(Les Brown)

Imagine that your child's brain is an old train with two steam engines at each end. The first points towards positive behaviour, which will allow the child to achieve their goals in life. The second engine points to a negative one, which will cause difficulties and suffering. Now I want you to imagine that every comment you make to your child is like a log. In which of the two fireboxes do you want to place the log? The one that fuels the locomotive towards satisfaction or towards dissatisfaction? Too often, frustrated parents focus all their attention on the negative behaviour of their children. This also happens at school. Some teachers, exasperated by children who don't collaborate, begin to focus their attention on the negative behaviour of the child. When we centre our attention on the negatives, we are placing a log in the firebox pointing towards difficulties. You may feel that your duty is to focus on everything negative your child does, so they will not do it again, but in many cases the only thing this does is fuel more bad behaviour. As you have seen in the previous chapter, the best strategy for encouraging positive behaviour in your child is to focus on their good behaviour. So how can we correct the negative behaviour in order to focus on the positive? By looking for alternatives to punishment.

Why punishment does not work

Punishing a child, either by taking away their bicycle or calling them a scaredy-cat or whiny, has three negative consequences that every parent and educator should avoid. Firstly, it teaches the child that using punishment against others is a valid form of conducting a relationship: what good does it do for the child to be called whiny? What advantage is there for the child, or the world, that they cannot enjoy time on their bike? Perhaps none at all. The only thing the child will learn is that they can lash out at others when

DOI: 10.4324/9781003360117-13

they are frustrated, and when the other person is made to feel bad, part of the damage they caused has been repaired. I don't know how you value these two assumptions, but they are not the values that I want to teach my children. The second negative consequence of punishing your child is that it facilitates guilt. The punishment will usually come to an end when the child starts to cry, or when enough time has passed for them to feel bad. When the child begins to cry or when their dignity is lost and they ask for forgiveness, the parent usually retracts the punishment. This is how the child will quickly learn that when they feel sad for doing something they should not have done, the parents forgive them and love them again.

This mechanism, so simple yet so terrible, is the origin of a child's guilt and it can accompany them throughout their entire lives. As if that weren't enough, the punishment does not prevent the child from unlearning what they learned through behaving badly. In other words, a child who hits another child won't stop feeling the satisfaction of having hit them. This is why limits are much more effective, as they prevent bad behaviour from occurring. In short, the child who is punished because they have misbehaved can create associations that provide little benefit to their development, as we will see in the following diagram.

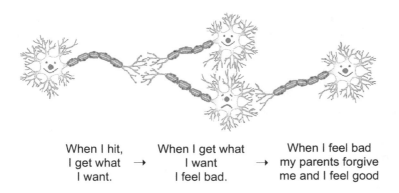

| When I hit, I get what I want. | → | When I get what I want I feel bad. | → | When I feel bad my parents forgive me and I feel good |

The last, and in my view the most negative, consequence of punishment, is what it tells the child about themselves. When we punish the child for not obeying us, or if we call them disobedient, their brain uses that information to form a "self-concept". Every time we say any phrase that begins with "you are", the child's brain stores that data in a structure called the "hippocampus", which is responsible for storing all knowledge about the world and about themselves, enabling them to make decisions in life. Therefore, if the child knows that a happy dog wags its tail, the child will want to stroke a dog whose tail is wagging. If the child knows that in summer people eat ice cream, they will ask their mum for an ice cream on a hot day to enjoy the cool taste of it. In the same way, if the child sees themselves as brave or obedient, they will act accordingly, while if the messages from parents or teachers have led the child to think that they are disobedient, they will also act accordingly. The child who knows they are disobedient, whiny, selfish or lazy will act in relation to what he or she knows about themselves. In this sense, there are few things that can do as much damage to self-concept and the child's possibilities, as all those negative messages that they have recorded in their memory about themselves.

Hippocampus

Knowledge of the world
- My teacher is called Sonia
- In summer we eat ice cream
- Dogs wag their tails when they are happy

Knowledge about themselves

- I'm a scaredy-cat
- I'm whiny
- I'm selfish

- I'm brave
- I'm able to wait
- I know how to share

Trick-punishments

Another reason that punishments may not be effective is due to what I call "trick-punishments". A trick-punishment is a reprimand, a moment of anger or a punishment in the most classic sense of the word. Instead of discouraging the child from doing something, it encourages them to do it. Trick-punishments appear when the child, usually one who does not receive enough attention from their parents, as they spend little time with their child and don't know how to reinforce positive behaviour, learns that they receive more attention by doing things wrong. For example, Hugh learns that when he hits his little brother, his mother scolds him. For a child who feels lonely, being scolded is much better than feeling invisible, so he will continue to hit his brother. In this case, his mother would be better adopting a different strategy. For example, she could congratulate Hugh when he has not hit his brother for a certain length of time. She could also spend a little time with Hugh every day, once she has put his little brother to bed. The mother clearly cannot allow the child to hit his little brother, but instead of constantly pointing out the negatives, she can choose to reward the positives. In this way, any parent can avoid trick-punishments; they can turn the situation on its head by focusing on the positives and not giving so much "prominence" to the negatives.

Trick-punishment

When I behave badly →
they pay attention to me.

Reinforcing the positive

When I behave well →
they pay attention to me.

As you can see, there are many reasons that make punishment a misguided strategy of educating children and it is one that prevents progress. Occasionally it may fulfil its purpose, but it always carries negative consequences. This doesn't, however, mean that I think we should allow the child to think they can do what they want. Punishing a child who has hit someone is probably much better than doing nothing. I simply mean that there are other strategies that are less harmful and more effective than punishment. In the following section we are going to take a look at them.

There are many alternatives to punishment that are going to help you to correct your children in a much more constructive and positive way than through punishment.

Help your child achieve it

The aim of all punishment is usually so you can help your child to learn and to achieve their goals. I want you to imagine that you are a cardiologist and that in a routine check-up you discover that your best friend has heart disease. If she doesn't start exercising and changing her diet she will have a heart attack, with negative repercussions for her health. What would you do in this situation? Would you wait for the heart attack to happen, and then reprimand her for the way she eats and her lack of exercise, or would you talk to her and help her to exercise more and eat more healthily? If you are a good friend, surely you wouldn't have to think twice about it. You would do anything to help your friend overcome her illness. With the added motivation that any good parent has, they should not wait for their child to fail; they should help them to achieve their goals and feel good. If you know that your son Sandy tends to bite his sister when he gets frustrated, don't wait for it to happen. Help Sandy avoid biting her. Sit close to him and when you see he is becoming frustrated, help him to control himself. If Steven does not come when his father calls him, he can sit there calling him, getting more and more angry, or he can choose to go up to Steven, take him gently by the hand and lead him to where he wanted him to go. The first method is a guarantee for mutual dissatisfaction. However, with just a little help, both father and son will feel better and be achieving their goals; the father will control the situation and Steven will go to where his father asked him to be. In the same way, if Rosie takes a long time to eat, we can choose to get angry, or we can help her finish sooner by cutting her meat into smaller pieces, helping her to eat it, or we could even allow her to leave a little food if she makes an effort to do most of the work.

Another advantage of helping the child not to get things wrong is that it helps what is called "learning without mistakes." This technique, designed to help learning in people who have memory issues, is based on the following premise: anyone can learn faster if they get it right the first time. If you help your child to do things well in situations where they usually fail, you are helping them to learn faster.

Establish consequences

In real life, each of our actions has a consequence. If we are late for a job interview, this may give a bad impression and we may not get the job. If we drive too fast, we might be fined, and if we put a lot of care into cooking, the food is more likely to taste delicious. When parents think about consequences, they immediately think of punishments. However, punishments are not usually necessary, as life provides the consequences needed to make the child understand what kind of behaviour offers them the best results. The job of the parents can therefore be as simple as showing the child the consequences of their actions, according to basic rules. Imagine that at Martin's house there are always arguments and raised voices, as he constantly leaves his toys scattered around his bedroom. His parents can establish the rule that he cannot take another toy out until he puts away the one he is not using. We are not punishing him by not allowing him to play; the child can hop around the house, do roly-polies or pretend to be a crocodile in the Amazon. However, he cannot take out another toy until he puts away the previous one. I remember some months ago my wife and I were becoming extremely impatient because one of our children was taking so long to have dinner. He would spend an hour and a half in front of a plate of vegetables, an omelette and a glass of milk. By the time he was ready to go to bed, we were too. He is not a disobedient child, nor does he have a small appetite; he simply likes to take his time; he enjoys inventing stories and talking non-stop. We wanted to help him finish within a reasonable time, but nothing worked. We spent months like this, trying to figure out how to help him, until one day we realised that if there was one thing he valued even more than chatting at the dinner table, it was his bedtime story. If we believed in punishments, we would have told him that there would be no bedtime story if he didn't finish within a certain time. Instead, we established a rule. The bedtime story would begin forty-five minutes after dinner had begun. It is an acceptable amount of time to have dinner without hurrying. We explained to the children that the story would begin at that time, whether they were in bed or not. The first night the rule went into effect, everything went on as usual, except for the fact that that evening I read *We are going on a Bear Hunt* on my own, lying in his bed, around forty-five minutes after they had started their dinner. Neither he nor his sister could believe it. They were very angry with me and cried, demanding that I read it again. As you can imagine, I refused. I knew that they would be able to overcome their frustration. The next day they ate their dinner in thirty-five minutes, we read the story of the bear, and then we read two more: a positive consequence of finishing early. From that evening on we began to read the story exactly forty-five minutes after sitting down at the table. Sometimes we would wait a minute or two because someone had forgotten to go to the toilet or had not brushed their teeth, but these days we are almost always on time for the bedtime story. You too can create some natural consequences for those tasks in which your children often get held up. The child should naturally adjust to these consequences, which as you can see, are much more effective and create less guilt than punishing them would.

Change the perspective

As you will remember from the previous chapter, reinforcement is much more effective than punishment, and this is why the following strategy is really useful. To be able to carry it out, you simply need to alter your own perspective on reward and punishment. Let's suppose Theresa is often annoying her sister. In this situation, many parents would establish a rule to stop her: "If Theresa keeps annoying her sister, she won't be allowed to watch cartoons after her snack." This is, to a certain extent, a fair outcome in the eyes of a child that age. However, more effective alternatives exist. If Theresa's parents apply this rule, they are focusing on Theresa annoying her sister, and this will cause frustration when the rule is broken. If we apply the changing perspective method, we can turn the situation around in a very similar way using a much more positive approach. The new rule could be: "Children who behave well at snack time will get to watch cartoons". The focus is now on good behaviour, and obeying the rule is associated with a feeling of satisfaction. It is a simple yet powerful idea, even though the most experienced parents can sometimes forget it. When establishing consequences, always try to apply them from a positive perspective. When you see that punishment is beginning to creep in more frequently, remember that you can turn it around and change the rule, so your child places all their attention (and therefore the part of the brain that controls their willpower) on positive behaviour.

Making amends

Another basic rule for correcting inappropriate behaviour is to make amends when harm to other people or objects has been caused. Making amends is a highly effective gesture of responsibility as it works as a natural consequence of their negative actions. I remember a mother who felt very overwhelmed, telling me that her son Michael took toys from his friends' houses.

She anxiously asked the parents of the other children if they had given the toy to her son and the usual answer was no. After she personally gave the toy back to the parents and apologised, I recommended the most natural thing: it was the child who should make amends. About a month later, I met up with this mum and asked her how everything was. She admitted that a few days after she had spoken to me, her son stole a few stickers from his friend's house. When they got home and his mother realised that the stickers were not his, she told the boy that he had to return them the next day, and say sorry for taking them. The following day, Michael kicked, cried and pleaded for his mother to return them. The mother, a very sweet and wise woman, told him that she would help him do it. Michael, who was a little calmer by that time, and felt braver with his mother by his side, returned the stickers and apologised. A few months have passed, and Michael has not taken any more toys from his friends' houses. Now he asks his mother to allow him to take some toys to his friends' house to exchange them for others, and always by mutual consent. Determining consequences is easier and less traumatic for children in general than how it was for Michael at that moment. When a child hits their sibling, correcting the damage means asking for forgiveness and giving their sibling a kiss. When they throw food on the floor, they can pick it up and put it in the bin, and when they spill milk while playing or while distracted, instead of telling the child off and saying that they should be more careful, we can help them look for a cloth and teach them how to wipe up the spilt milk. Their brain will learn how to be more careful with things and instead of being traumatic, it will be fun. But more importantly, as I say to my own children: "Why do I have to pick it up if you have the hands to do it, and I'm not the one to have dropped it?"

Remember

Punishment is the least pleasant and least educational consequence that can be applied to a child for their actions. Sometimes the child seeks confrontation or punishment because they need to feel that their parents are giving them attention.

It is very important to remember that all children need a lot of time to play and receive attention from their parents. Telling them off only punishes their needs and reinforces their bad behaviour. Look for effective alternatives to avoid entering into the dynamics of bad behaviour. Establish clear consequences, insist that they make amends for actions that hurt other people or cause damage to objects, and above all, help them to do things well when you think you will end up losing your temper. Remember that a good friend would not sit still waiting for you to go and greet them; they would walk to meet you halfway. You can also meet your child halfway and help them to accomplish what you are asking for. Instead of getting angry and frustrated, help your child to feel like a winner!

11

Establishing limits without drama

A disciplined mind leads to happiness, and an undisciplined mind leads to suffering.

(Attributed to Dalai Lama)

Limits have always been a controversial issue in education. All over the world there are educational trends and parents who are determined to reduce limits and rules to the bare minimum. The first ones to disagree with establishing limits in the educational process are the children themselves. There is no better way to see the darker side of any child than to establish a limit that the child hadn't taken into account. Even the sweetest child can become a little devil when facing the frustration of having to comply with a limit that did not previously exist. This is certainly why many parents and educators have a hard time setting limits and enforcing them. The panic caused by having to deal with an angry child, or the desperation caused by having to see their distress is such that educational theories have been developed based on minimising these limits. However, from my experience, and from the perspective of leading educators, this is a serious mistake.

From my point of view as a neuropsychologist, I can assure every parent and educator that limits are essential to brain education. I can support this statement as there is an entire area of the brain devoted exclusively to establishing limits, enforcing them, and helping people to cope with the frustration of complying with them. Moreover, this part of the brain, known as the "prefrontal" region, is undoubtedly the most important in achieving happiness. When I meet a patient who has damaged this part of their brain, I am seeing a person who is not able to regulate their anger, who does not respect other people's limits, and who cannot comply with social norms in order to achieve their goals. Human brains have spent millions of years developing these boundary-setting structures, as they improve – both in years gone by and nowadays – their chances of surviving and living together in society.

DOI: 10.4324/9781003360117-14

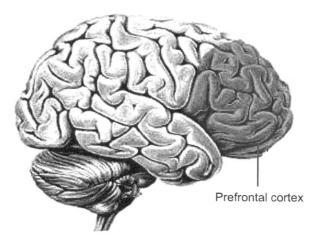

Prefrontal cortex
- Internalising rules
- Self-control
- Planning
- Organising
- Problem solving
- Detecting faults

Prefrontal cortex

Some parents insist on stigmatising the establishment of limits without realising that, by consenting to the child in every situation, it is incongruous. Parents also have to set limits on their own needs and desires so that their child can experience life's standard limits. Let's look at the example of breast (or bottle) feeding, since it is perhaps the most controversial. From the time the child is three or four months old, they are able to wait calmly for short periods of time before being fed. This means that to some extent the mother can regulate the baby's intake. If you are going to drive somewhere, you can offer the baby milk before getting in the car, so they don't need to feed while you are driving. In the same way, if the mother is in the queue for the bus, she can quietly wait to be seated inside the bus comfortably in order to fulfil the child's needs. Without a doubt, feeding on demand is the best option for raising a baby, but this is also compatible with wanting to teach your baby that in certain situations he or she can wait a little.

In the field of education, limits are fundamental to your child's development. We know that their ability to set their own limits and be able to control themselves is the best indicator of academic and social success. You just have to speak to a group of teachers to understand that children nowadays need limits, even more than love or affection. Even something as widespread as attention deficit disorder is largely caused by a lack of limits. We will talk later about how limits can help in the child's intellectual and emotional development and how they can contribute to preventing attention deficit disorder and other pathologies. I hope you have now convinced yourself of how important it is for your child's brain to know how to internalise and respect limits, as we now look at exactly how to establish and enforce these. And to do so with no drama for you or the child.

The attitude for setting limits

I want you to imagine a scene that you have possibly already experienced: a baby of around one year of age gets into the cupboard under the sink. The baby sits, opens the door, and discovers a fascinating world of detergents, bleaches and dishwasher tablets. What would you do in this situation? Without a moment's hesitation, you would remove the product from the child's hands, close the door and move the child away from the cupboard. Would you not? Great. Now I want you to record this scene in your mind and to clearly remember the feeling of calm that came over you when you removed the imaginary bottle of bleach from your child's hands. Setting limits effectively and without dramas requires this very attitude. The attitude of knowing that what you are doing is good for your child – the attitude that there is no discussion necessary, and of being certain of how the scene will end. When your child is about to hit another child, when they are going to jump from somewhere high, or when they decide that they want to eat without their bib, your attitude should just be as immediate, clear and safe as when you grab that bottle of detergent. In simple terms; whatever it is that you don't want to happen, don't let it happen.

Setting limits on inappropriate behaviour is very important because we are preventing connections being formed between neurons that will not encourage their intellectual, emotional and social development. Let's look at an example. If a child wants another child's toy, they may decide to hit that child in order to get it. In this case, the child feels the satisfaction of having got what they wanted, although in doing it, they have violated a very important social rule. If on the other hand, we set a limit to ensure that the child keeps his or her toy, we avoid a connection being made and consequently the child repeating the behaviour.

Without limits
When I hit →
I get what I want.
I'm going to keep hitting.

With limits
When I hit →
I don't get what I want.
I won't hit again.

In setting limits, we are not only putting a stop to unwanted behaviour and therefore helping to improve the child's self-control, we are also making it easier for the child to look for other alternatives, thus making the child more flexible and adaptable.

When to start setting limits

Many parents do not realise that limits are part of the child's life from the moment they are born, and it is important that they get used to them gradually. When a baby is in the womb, it knows no limits at all. They are at one with their mother and there are no barriers that separate them. The fusion and infinite placidity that we feel in the placenta is perhaps what makes it hard for many adults to accept limits. However, it is the rule of life. Outside the womb, things are no longer the same. If everything goes well during childbirth and the baby and mother are lucky enough to stay together, skin to skin, for the first few hours after birth, the initial separation between the child and its mother will be when the mother has to go to the toilet, and a little later when she has to take a shower. During these moments, the mother cannot be with the child, and from then on there will be many other moments in which, however much the baby objects, it will not get what it wants. During these initial moments, these limits are unavoidable.

The time for the parent to have to set limits on the child is usually when the baby begins to move around more. You may have your baby in your arms, and she tries to throw herself on the floor, or just turn over again and again when you try to change her nappy. When this happens, it is important to remember the bleach bottle rule. Do you think it is good for the child to throw herself on the floor? Do you think it is possible to change your baby's nappy when she is turning over? If the answer to these two questions is a no, I recommend that you pick up your child calmly and affectionately, but with assurance, in the same way you would with the bleach bottle. Of course you can have endless moments of fun seeing how she turns over, how she investigates something she saw on the floor, but if at that moment you really need to put her nappy on or take her somewhere, try holding your child firmly and calmly, and gently say to them: "Not now" or "Just a minute". In this way you are getting your child to make associations that will help them throughout their life.

Even though I want something now
...I'm able to wait a little while.

Later in the book you will learn how important it is for the child's brain to know how to wait. For the moment we'll concentrate on it being crucial for their emotional and intellectual development.

Sometimes limits are not as simple as asking the child to wait a little to be able to do what they want. There are also many occasions, especially as the child grows older, in which we must replace "Not now" with "No". However, the principle of applying it is the same. The more secure, clear, calm and affectionate you are when it comes to saying "no", the easier it will be for your child to understand. Suppose your son has finished breakfast early and wants to watch cartoons before school. He sneaks into the living room and turns on the television. There is a very clear rule in your house that on school days children are not allowed to watch television in the morning. Yes, your son has woken up early and finished his breakfast in no time, but there has been no alteration to the rule. In this case, you can turn off the television without saying anything, or approach the situation with love, acknowledge that he has eaten his breakfast very well and explain that he is not allowed to watch television. You can, however, sit with him for five minutes to read a story. As you see, although the limit has been respected in both cases, the way in which it is put into effect can have very different consequences. In the first case there will most likely be an outburst of anger towards you, while in the second case he will probably respect your decision and accept it willingly. What I wish to convey here is that there are many ways to enforce limits. While some may cause fits of temper and a deterioration in your relationship with your children, others can prevent conflicts and help to build mutual trust. This next section will describe what I call "the seven golden rules for setting limits successfully". In other words, how to set limits so the child is able to understand and internalise them, and how avoid making it a traumatic experience (for either of you)

The seven rules for setting limits without dramas

- *Early.* If you set a limit the first time you observe behaviour that you don't like or don't think is appropriate, you will avoid a negative first connection in the child's brain. This means you will have much less work to do in the future because you will be preventing negative behaviour from developing further.
- *Before.* When you see that your child is about to do something that you consider dangerous or negative for their development, try to stop it before it happens. As with the previous rule, avoiding unwanted behaviour before it occurs can be much more effective than correcting it twenty times once the child has acquired the habit. It will save you a lot of work.
- *Always.* Getting a child to give up inappropriate behaviour does not mean that they will not try it again. Children are curious and persistent by nature. The key to the limits being enforced is that they are clear and present in your brain at all times.
- *Consistently.* It is no help if the child's father does not let her watch cartoons in the morning and her mother sometimes allows it. It is vital that you and your partner agree on what standards and rules are important for your child's development.
- *Calmly.* Part of the secret of effectively setting limits is to do so in a calm manner. When we shout at a child, or when we become agitated,

it activates a part of the brain which practically disables the cerebral cortex area that controls the management of limits. In these instances, the child will not be able to listen, understand or learn what you are trying to teach them.

- *With trust.* One of the most important things when leading someone is for that person to trust that we know where we are leading them. If your child sees that you are clear about what they can and cannot do, they will feel calmer and more motivated when following the rules that you have set. There will be less discussion over it because they will know that it will not be easy to change your mind.
- *With love.* When a limit is set with love, the child fully understands that it is not an attack against them, it is simply a rule that must be followed. Their level of frustration will be considerably less, and you will be able to enforce the limit without your relationship suffering as a consequence.

As you can see, setting limits does not have to be tumultuous. You can even make it fun. If Paul runs away when we want him to put his shoes on, we can say: "Hey, you rascal!", grab him by the ankles and joke that he won't be able to escape until he puts his shoes on. If Megan throws something on the floor and doesn't want to pick it up, you can look at her sternly, but you can also push her to the floor and tickle her, saying "you little scoundrel!" and finish the game by picking up what she threw on the floor. The secret of setting limits is not to make a scene, but to get the child to act in the way that we have shown them. Adding laughter to the moment will lower the tension, prevent the child from feeling guilty and help them to accomplish what you are asking. As well as this, it can be an excellent opportunity to play and to strengthen your bond, rather than eroding it.

Different types of limits

At some point or other, you may be thinking that limits are a bit cold and rigid; that standards set at home are hard and fast rules that cannot be broken under any circumstances. Nothing could be further from the truth. So far, I have aimed to show you how to set the limits when you want to, although there is another important aspect that must be taken into consideration when setting limits: the need of the child to achieve their own goals. Can you imagine how a child would feel if they never ever got their own way? They would probably feel very insecure. Teaching a child to understand and to respect the rules is just as important as providing them with experiences in which they achieve a positive result when the odds are set against them. In this sense, it is as important to know how to enforce limits as to know how to break them. I recently heard of a way to classify limits that I found very accurate. It closely resembles the standard classification that many parents do unconsciously. I believe that understanding these limits and giving them a name will help many parents to manage them more effectively in the real world.

- *Unbreakable rules.* Those which are essential for guaranteeing the child's safety. Don't put your fingers in the socket, we hold hands when crossing the road, you cannot climb too high on your own, do not drink the bottle of bleach, and many others that fall within the realm of common sense, that almost all parents do very well.
- *Important limits for their wellbeing.* Those limits that must always be put in place, or almost always, since they are important for the child's development and wellbeing. However, a few exceptions or alterations can be made. For example, you can explain to a child that they should not hit another child, although you can reaffirm their right to defend themselves if someone attacks them. It is also important that they have lunch and dinner every day, but if the child has a sore tummy, the logical thing is for them not to eat anything. Many of these limits are to do with parental values and social norms. No hitting; no spitting; no telling lies; no swearwords; sweets can't be eaten all the time; breakfast, lunch and dinner must always be eaten, etc.
- *Important limits for living together.* Limits which are usually established by parents to help everyone coexist in a peaceful, orderly way. They are rules that must be respected, although parents can relax them at the weekend, during holidays, when guests are over, or when we need to break the rule through necessity (and sometimes simply because we want to give the child the satisfaction of getting away with it). For example: the child has to have a bath every day, they can't eat in the living room, they aren't allowed ice cream after dinner, they can only have sweets at the weekend, they can only watch an hour of cartoons each day, and they have to brush their teeth.

Establishing limits that the child can break when we let them will teach them that they can (and have to) be flexible in life. It will also teach them that rules can change depending on the circumstances, as well as allowing us to have a more adaptable family life. If on a Saturday night we decided to stay at granny and grandpa's house after spending the day there, we won't be able to brush our teeth or get into our pyjamas before bed. Breaking the rules will help our children's brains learn that having a fun evening with granny, playing with farm animals, has more value than closely following every rule at all times.

In the previous three chapters you have learnt three tools that can help you motivate your child and help them to understand which behaviour is appropriate and which is inappropriate. You may have read – or a friend has told you – that setting limits or reinforcing children is not a good strategy. Well, neuroscience has a different opinion to that of your friend, as each of these tools is indeed useful and allows the child to establish a series of rules that are very important for their development. It is, without a doubt, your responsibility as a parent to teach your children how far they can go and how they can get what they want in life. The best thing about limits and reinforcements is that if they are applied effectively from the beginning, the child's brain will quickly secure the relevant habits that will allow you to keep progressing, instead of forcing you to continue fighting over the same issues again and again.

Remember

Helping the child to understand and respect limits is one of the most important tasks that any parent has in encouraging the intellectual and emotional development of their children.

Don't feel guilty about setting limits. Limits are there from birth and are part of everyone's lives. Try to set the limits before the behaviour occurs, or at least before it becomes a habit. Set limits with the same firmness, tranquillity and affection with which you give your children a kiss. As you will see later, you will be helping them to develop a part of their brain which will enable them to achieve their goals and to be happy throughout their lives.

12

Communication

The most influential of all educational factors is the conversation in a child's home.

(William Temple)

Good communication is what allows two people to connect with each other. In the communication that takes place between parents and children, good communication is what helps the child to connect ideas, emotions and thinking styles. If you were hoping to discover complex techniques and exercises to stimulate your children's brains, I'm happy to tell you that getting into your child's mind is much easier than you think. Every day, in kitchens, bedrooms and bathrooms in millions of homes all around the world, mums and dads work the miracle of helping their children establish neural connections to develop their intellectual and emotional capacity. To achieve this, they use a tool that is as simple as it is effective: communication.

Thanks to an infinite number of studies, we know that communication between parents and children is the main route of intellectual development during the first years of life. Memory, concentration, abstraction, knowledge of the environment, self-regulation, and language itself, need communication to flourish. The child's brain is programmed to learn and acquire all the intellectual abilities characteristic of human beings, but without encouragement and conversation from their parents, they will never fully develop. For example, the ability to understand and utter words is something innate to any person, yet a child cannot develop it by themselves; they need adult stimulus to be able to acquire this tool. Neither Cervantes nor Shakespeare could have written their celebrated works if they had not first learnt to speak with the help of their parent. Intelligence is another skill that is developed mainly through conversations between parents and children. If Einstein had been raised by a troop of chimpanzees, he would never have been able to learn to speak, and his unlimited ability of reason would have been lost in the limited universe of tree branches and bananas.

DOI: 10.4324/9781003360117-15

Throughout the book you can see examples of effective ways of communicating; communicative styles that encourage collaboration, promote mutual trust, stimulate a more organised memory or help the child to develop positive thinking. In previous chapters you have seen how communicating with empathy, that which reinforces positive behaviour and which sets limits using love, can be useful for the child to internalise social norms and to know how to calm their mood when they are flustered. In this chapter we are going to focus on a very specific communication technique, which will allow you to connect more effectively with your child's brain. If you use this very simple technique, it will be easier to guide your child, as its principal virtue is to encourage the child to collaborate with the adult.

Cooperative communication

I am going to ask you to picture a common situation that sometimes happens with your partner. The kitchen is a mess and it's your turn to tidy up. However, you can't be bothered and quite frankly, you don't feel like tidying up. I want you to read these two examples and choose in which of the two cases you would be more likely to cooperate with what your partner is asking you.

Example A

"The kitchen is a complete pigsty. I've been waiting for you to clean it for half an hour and you haven't done a thing about it. You're just sitting there watching television. Go and get it cleaned up right now."

Example B

"Darling, have you seen the state of the kitchen? I'm a bit stressed out because there aren't even any plates we can use for our dinner. Will you switch off the television and we can clean it up together? Will you give me a hand?"

The first example reflects a questioning communication style. The second is an example of what I call "cooperative communication". Cooperative or collaborative communication is a style of communication that comes from research done by Elaine Rees, Robyn Fivush and other scientists who study communication between parents and children. This style of communication increases the chance of the child collaborating with the adult in any task that they propose. It can be used when we want the child to sit at the table for dinner, tidy up the playroom or simply listen to us more carefully when we are explaining something to them. It is a widespread communication technique among professionals who work with people with intellectual disabilities, including those who work with children with behavioural problems, attention deficit disorders, or cognitive difficulties. The reason why it is so widespread is that, regardless of the communication style that each person has developed throughout their lives, we know that this style of communication can be taught through training. Many professionals do just this, and there have also been studies in which, through training different groups of parents in techniques that are similar to those I am going to show you now, communication between parents and children is improved.

Cooperative communication is not an infallible technique – there is always the possibility that the child does not want to collaborate – but this style of communication greatly promotes the child's collaboration with the adult. However, its main virtue is not to get the child to collaborate more effectively, but to facilitate a connection with the adult's thinking. Below, you can read a brief description of the four most characteristic elements of this form of communication.

Turn a task into teamwork

The effectiveness of cooperative communication lies in asking the child to collaborate in turning tasks into teamwork. When the child feels accompanied, the task seems more enjoyable and simpler than when they have to do it alone. Female friends go to the bathroom together, boys prefer to go and talk to girls in a group and parents join school associations to make improvements in the education of their children. We are all more willing to undertake a task that seems somewhat difficult if we feel accompanied. For the child, "take off your clothes" sounds much more difficult and lonelier than "let's take our clothes off". It is just the way you say it. You don't actually have to take your clothes off, simply give the message to the child in such a way that their brain understands that it will be something that is easy to do.

Ask them to collaborate

The second advantage of cooperative communication is that when the child understands that the adult is asking for collaboration, the probability of a positive response increases. The explanation of this phenomenon is very simple. Human beings are social beings. They like to feel accompanied and enjoy receiving help and offering their help to others. It's in our genes. Some studies show that from the age of one and a half years, we feel the urge to help those who are in need. A child of that age is able to bring objects to a person that cannot reach them, and as they get older they begin to comfort those who are sad and help others whenever they can or are asked to. This tendency is also much stronger among members of the same family. Your child wants to help you, they want to be with you, and this will make it more likely that they pay attention to you if you ask for it, offering collaboration. If you want your child to tidy away their toys, instead of saying "Pick up your toys", try asking them: "Can you help me tidy them away?"

Help them to think

Sometimes children find it hard to collaborate simply because they are not thinking the same as their parents. One evening, the time might be flying by, they have not yet had dinner, and you promised to read them a very special bedtime story. You may start to get agitated and ask the children to hurry up, when they are perfectly happy messing about with their food. In cases such as this, focusing the attention on your own worries can be very useful. You can say things like, "We need to be careful, it's getting a little late and if we don't hurry up, we're not going to get to school", "Look, your little brother is very tired because he hasn't had his nap, so don't play with him at the moment as he is crying over everything". You can also ask the child questions that allow them to feel what you are feeling, such as: "How do you think we could fix this?", or "What do you think?". If you manage to involve the child in your thinking process, they will be more able to understand what you are feeling and what you need from them. Therefore, they will be more likely to collaborate with you.

Offer them freedom

I know that to many parents this might seem strange, but the truth is that the child is more likely to do what we ask them if we allow them a certain degree of freedom instead of ordering them to do things. All of us like to feel that we have choice, and we get angry when we feel forced to do something. The same thing happens with children. They collaborate more effectively when we offer them freedom. Part of the trick is that when they decide what they want to do, they cannot get angry or argue with you, and they also collaborate better, as offering them freedom helps them to feel respected and valued. Instead of saying, "You have to put your dirty clothes in the basket and put your pyjamas on", try asking, "What would you like to do first: put your pyjamas on, or throw your dirty clothes into the basket?" In this way, a situation that is usually difficult for a child turns into a positive moment. You can let them choose between eating their soup first, or their fish, brushing their teeth with the children's toothpaste or the grownups' toothpaste, having a bath or taking a shower, and many more options that will help your child collaborate better and learn to make their own decisions.

Remember

Different communication styles can provide better or worse results when it comes to getting a child to collaborate with an adult. The most effective communication style is one that turns tasks into teamwork that requires collaboration. This involves the child in the adult's thought processes and allows them to feel part of the decision making. Cooperative communication is not an infallible method, but even so, it significantly increases the probability that the child will put themselves in the shoes of the adult and collaborate with them.

Part III

Emotional intelligence

13

Teach emotional intelligence

Emotions have taught mankind to reason.

(Luc de Clapiers)

As you will have already seen through their looks, smiles, cries and tantrums, the child's brain is something much more tender and emotional than a computer. The emotional brain has an undeniable importance in the child, who functions in terms of excitement, anger, desire and fear. Understanding their emotions and learning how to access them and how to support their emotional development is therefore highly advantageous for those parents who know how to do it.

The importance of the emotional brain goes far beyond its role in the first six years of life and in the relationship between parents and children throughout this period. Thanks to considerable research of late, we know that the emotional brain plays a crucial role in the lives of adults. Let's use you, the reader, as an example. Obviously I don't know you, but I can't imagine you didn't feel intensely emotional when your newborn child opened their eyes and looked up at you for the first time, when your baby wraps their tiny hand around your finger, when they take their first steps, or when your child falls asleep in your arms. The moment a child comes into our lives, parents are exposed to a melting pot of emotions. In these precious moments the emotional impact is clear, but few people understand the influence of their emotional brain in other aspects of their life.

The emotional brain is present in all actions of your daily life. Every time you buy a product, every morning when you choose a seat on public transport, or every afternoon when you decide what you are going to have for dinner, your emotional brain is letting you know how it feels with each different alternative. Far from being overwhelmed by the most important decisions in life, whether it is choosing a person to share your life with, planning a project at work, or deciding whether to buy a house, the emotional brain grows and asserts a powerful, sometimes unstoppable influence on the rational brain. We know that the biggest decisions we make in our lives are

DOI: 10.4324/9781003360117-17

those based on emotion, and only a small percentage of them on reason. In this sense, emotions are like the dark matter of the universe: they can often not be seen, but they account for 70% of our brain's energy.

If there is one concept to have transcended the realm of psychology and entered into our everyday lives over the last decades, it is that every human being is equipped with emotional intelligence, in addition to a formal or rational intelligence. Since Daniel Goleman published his famous book, *Emotional Intelligence*, the popularity of the concept and its applications have continued to grow. According to Goleman, just as there is a rational intelligence that we use to solve problems of logic, there is an emotional one that helps us to achieve our goals and feel good about ourselves and others. As you have already learnt, the human brain has a processing area that we call the "emotional brain" which is responsible for the person's emotional side. One of the main contributions of emotional intelligence has been to place value on people's feelings and emotions. Experiencing wellbeing is finally now seen as a sign of intelligence, which is just as important as being able to solve a complex mathematical problem.

After years of research we now know that people with greater emotional intelligence are not only happier, but they also make better decisions, have more success in business and make more effective leaders. In any area of life in which you have to deal with others, emotional intelligence offers a big advantage. In my own home we place a lot of value on a balanced brain development, but as far as education is concerned, my wife and I have a weakness for the emotional side. It is not that we are "softer", we simply choose to give priority to the emotional development of our children, in part because our values lead us to think like this, but also because as a neuropsychologist I know that the entire intellectual brain is built on the emotional brain.

Now that you know the importance of emotional intelligence both for the wellbeing of the child and for their ability to interact with other people and achieve their goals, I am sure that you will want to know how to support the development of your child's emotional brain. In this third part of the book, we will explore together some components of this intelligence and learn the principles and strategies that will allow you to feed your child's emotional brain.

14

Bonds

Childhood is the garden where we will play as grownups.

(Anonymous)

When psychologists talk about "bonds", we are referring to the relationship the child establishes with their parents and the world around them. A child's world is small. Any child knows that their mother is the prettiest, the kindest, and the cleverest, and that their dad is the strongest and bravest dad in the whole world. For a child, his or her parents are heaven and Earth; their point of reference in the universe. Based on them, they create an image of what the world around them is like. If you have loving parents, you will see the world as a good and safe place. If either of them is excessively authoritarian, hard on you, or demanding, you may feel worthless, or that your problems are not important. You may also find it difficult to feel satisfied with yourself and others. For many psychologists, the bond established between parents and children is the key to self-esteem. When a child feels safe and unconditionally loved, they grow up feeling valued and that they deserve to feel happy. Helping your child to have a high level of self-esteem is offering them the possibility of a happy life. Think about it; the world is full of people who have everything and who feel miserable. You can have a good job, friends, an incredible partner, lots of money or a wonderful family, but if you don't value yourself, if you don't love yourself, nothing you have achieved will matter because it won't make you feel truly happy. From my point of view, there is nothing more important than helping a child feel good about themselves and that is why in this chapter we will explore the key elements for building a relationship with your child that allows them to develop a high level of self-esteem.

We understand the importance of this bond thanks to research performed by American psychologist, Harry Harlow. Dr Harlow arrived at the University of Wisconsin with the sole purpose of deepening the learning processes during childhood. In order to achieve this, he decided to study macaques, as they are much more similar to human beings than the classic laboratory rat.

DOI: 10.4324/9781003360117-18

As in any experiment, one of the most important aspects is to have all the variables controlled; this is why Dr Harlow decided to build cages that were all exactly the same, apply strict schedules of light and dark, provide identical food and drink rations and, to avoid uncontrollable influences from their mothers, he separated all the macaque babies from their mothers at exactly the same time. Although Harlow only needed the macaque babies to perform several learning tests, he quickly realised that something was wrong. The monkeys, deprived of maternal contact, began to show serious psychological problems. More than a third of them gathered together in a corner of the cage and were listless and sad. Another third developed aggressive behaviour: they attacked their caregivers and other monkeys, and were anxious, incessantly moving around their cage. The others simply died of anguish or sorrow. This finding was so important that Harlow devoted the rest of his career to studying the importance of attachment. In one of his most famous studies he offered monkeys who could not see their mothers a rag doll to spend the night with. Fascinatingly, these monkeys slept while hugging their rag doll and barely experienced any psychological problems. Perhaps even more revealing was his following experiment, which was carried out to check the strength of this need for attachment. Each night, Harlow offered the monkeys the chance to sleep in one of two cages: the first contained a doll made of wire which held a bottle of warm milk. In the second, there was only their *own* rag doll. Even though the monkeys had not eaten anything for hours, each day the babies chose to give up food and spend the night with their rag doll mummy.

There have been many investigations that have studied the importance of bonds in a child's development. But after hearing of the experiments carried out with the monkeys, I am sure that you now understand the critical importance of the relationship between mother and child for a healthy development of the emotional brain. It could be said that this feeling of security which a child gets from being in its parent's arms is the foundation on which all emotional development is based. Without a bond of trust and security, the child may have serious difficulties in relating to others and the outside world.

In this sense, the truth is that your child is privileged. Previous generations did not know the importance of attachment for healthy emotional development. When you were brought up by your parents, there was not such a clear conscience regarding this issue, partly because when they themselves were brought up, the concept was completely the opposite. When your grandparents raised your parents, the most widespread trend in child rearing dictated that parents had a responsibility to strengthen their children's character. Forging a child's character was all about discipline, a heavy hand and meagre rations of love. Many went to boarding schools when they were very young and in traditional households fathers, who at that time were more authoritarian, berated mothers who were overly affectionate. Fortunately, times have changed and today we know a lot about how you can help your children develop a bond of trust and security with the world.

The attachment hormone

The true union of a family is not built on blood ties, but on love and mutual respect. For the child, attachment begins in the womb. We know that from the sixth month of pregnancy the foetus can recognise the voice of the mother, although it is just after birth when the baby experiences its first moment of separation. Until then the baby and the mother were one, and therefore the baby did not need to feel that it existed. The truth is that the moment of childbirth can be a very different experience for the baby and for the mother. The mother has read books, attended courses, has shared her excitement with her partner and, above all, has waited for months to meet her child. The baby, meanwhile, has no idea what is about to happen. It is not waiting for anyone, nor does it have a feeling of excitement, built up over months, to meet someone special. However, they are joined by a common experience: the strongest sensation of togetherness that two human beings can experience. Forget about the moment when you thought that if your girlfriend left you, you would die, or when you felt so connected to your partner because he included all your favourite songs in that CD. The union between the baby and the mother is unequalled, and part of the magic of the bond at the time of birth is the work of a hormone: oxytocin – a hormone that is produced during childbirth and that, among other things, allows women to endure the pain of childbirth. What you may not know is that it is also the hormone of love, and that during the delivery and the hours afterwards, the levels of oxytocin in your brain and in that of your baby reach their peak. This allows the creation of a unique sensation of union between baby and mother. During the following months, mother and child will share moments of great intimacy and physical contact, especially when the child breastfeeds or takes a bottle, when the mother holds the baby in her arms, shares a look or when the sweet words of the mother gently reach the baby's ears. While this is happening, fathers can also build their own bond with their child by changing nappies, dressing them and having the responsibility of giving the baby a bath every day. The physical contact and the glances they will share will strengthen and fortify that union, which, if taken care of properly, will last a lifetime.

Create a secure environment

The baby feels safe when its brain knows what is going to happen. Routines help a baby to feel calm and safe. Trying to follow more or less the same daily routine for dressing, feeding, bathing or putting them to sleep will help them be calmer, eat better and get used to sleep habits more quickly.

Being consistent with the physical spaces and even with the words we use during the first few months when we change, dress or put our baby to bed will also help them feel more secure. It is not necessary, nor is it advisable to be too strict with your routines. For the child, it is equally as important to know that their environment is safe, as it is to learn to be flexible and adapt to changes. Calm, flexible routines help the child feel tranquil and safe in different situations. Rigid routines, on the other hand, can make their brain feel insecure in the face of any small change.

Take care of their needs

Stereotypes, television adverts, and Hollywood films allow us to think that we should take them on holiday to Disneyland or shower them with treats and toys to be able to create a unique relationship with them. Nothing is further from the truth. Along with physical contact, the most basic care that mothers and fathers give their children is the main way to build attachment. Feeding, preparing food, getting them dressed, cleaned, bathed, taking them to school or the paediatrician; in short, taking care of the child's needs is essential in order to provide a sense of security and attachment. Although it may seem somewhat material, this type of care is fundamental to their survival. A child cannot satisfy their own needs by themselves, so their brain identifies and generates attachment with those who provide it. In this sense, it is important that both fathers and mothers take care of children personally, because it is through the simplest gestures of care that the child builds a relationship of love and safety towards their parents and the world around them.

Keep looking for physical contact

Gradually the baby gets older. They are able to walk longer distances without asking to be carried, they are becoming more autonomous with their food and sleep habits, and they can even spend time playing with other children without turning to you. Can you imagine the day they no longer give you a kiss? The day that they feel such detachment from you, that they don't want to bring your grandchildren to visit you? Surely you don't even want to think about it. Every parent dreams of having a special lifelong relationship with their children. Achieving it is as simple as continuing to build that bond throughout your lives. As it grows, the child's brain still needs the presence of the parent in the form of oxytocin. In truth, we all need to be close to each other to feel safe. Who doesn't like a hug?

You can do many things to avoid losing physical contact and continue building that bond that you have always dreamt of having with your child. Every time you hold your child in your arms, you brush their hair, hug them or take them to school holding hands, your brains generate oxytocin, which makes you ever more united. Helping each other and supporting each other also generates oxytocin, but there is nothing like physical contact to generate that union, that bond of trust with one another, and one of the best ways to achieve this is by playing with them. Lie on the floor and allow your children to climb on top of you, squeeze and hug you. Invent games where you can play at grabbing, punching and biting each other. My children's favourite game is that of the Cuddle-a-saurus, in which their father becomes a scary dinosaur who only wants to give his children cuddles. Sit them on your lap to read lots and lots of stories to them, and cultivate the expression of affection by giving them a kiss and a hug every time you drop them off at school or leave home to go to work. Those little gestures are the bricks on which you can build the palace of your future relationship.

Create reciprocal conversations

All parents want their children to share their experiences, worries and dreams with them. Many parents ask their children to tell them absolutely everything when they come home from school. By the time the child is six years old, he or she will have grown tired of "informing" their mother about everything they have done, or what has gone on throughout the day. Nobody likes to be interrogated or feel that they are the only one who has to share their private thoughts. Instead of "interrogating" your child, a more effective strategy is to aim for reciprocal communication. It is simple to do; you just have to share your own experiences, worries and dreams. When you arrive at school to pick up your children, when you get home or when you sit down to dinner, you can break the ice by telling them a little story from your day. It doesn't need to be anything special; it can be something as simple as "Today at work I had pasta for lunch", or "This morning on the way to work I saw a dog that was *this* big!". If you share extraordinary experiences with your children, your child will act in a reciprocal way. As well as sharing your day-to-day with them, if you are able to get into their world and spend time talking about the things that really interest them, such as their favourite cartoon characters or the names of their dolls, your child will really enjoy talking to you because they will know that it is a fair and reciprocal relationship.

The island of detachment

In the chapter dedicated to empathy, we spoke about the "insula": a region of the brain, hidden between two folds, that is fundamental to the dialogue between the rational and emotional brain. One of the main tasks of the insula is to understand and make sense of unpleasant sensations; it quickly activates when it comes across repulsive odours or tastes, such as when we smell or taste something which has gone off. When this region is activated, we experience a feeling of disgust. We immediately turn our head, wrinkle up our nose to close the olfactory pathways and stick out our tongue to expel the bad taste from our mouth. The most peculiar thing about the insula, and the reason why I have brought it up, is that a few years ago we discovered that this region is activated in a similar way when a child or adult perceives a falsehood or injustice. It seems reasonable: the sense of disgust that separates us from what can be harmful to our body, is similar to the feeling of distrust that separates us from someone who can cause us psychological harm.

Everyone knows that lying is bad. However, many parents resort to fibbing in order to get their children to sleep, finish their meal or do what they tell them. They can use old tricks like the bogeyman or tell fibs like saying to your child that the shop is closed, when actually you can't be bothered to go and buy the doll you promised them. If you want to keep your children close to you and help them trust themselves and the outside world, keep your word and don't use fibs to get what you want. The brain cannot remain close to someone who lies or who doesn't keep their word. It generates repulsion and distrust. In the parent–child relationship, not keeping your word or lying to them will result in the child psychologically moving away from their parents. On the other hand, parents who don't tell fibs and who keep their word, manage to create lasting bonds. Not only that, in some studies it has been shown that the probability of a child doing what they are asked is double when the person asking for something is someone that the child considers trustworthy because they keep their word. A good policy for all those parents who want to create a unique and lasting relationship with their children is simply to keep your word; make an effort to respect what you have agreed on and make keeping promises a priority. To achieve this, you just have to follow a simple rule. Do not promise anything you cannot deliver and do not go back on what you have promised.

Make them feel valued

Sometimes children can find their parents really annoying in their day-to-day lives. "Finish your milk", "Put your shoes on", "Don't hit your brother", "Keep your shoes on", "Turn off the television", and so on. Surely any relationship in which one of the two parties spends the day giving orders or instructions to the other has little future. I'm sure you think your son or daughter is a wonderful person. This is why it is important for this message to be expressed and more present in your conversations than whether or not they have put their shoes on. This is why I am going to share a principle that all parents should follow with their children.

> At the end of the day, the number of positive comments you give to your children should far outweigh the number of orders, instructions or negative comments.

When I knew I was going to be a father, I wondered how I would be able to enjoy fatherhood to the full. Immediately an image came to my mind: that of my children rushing out to meet me at the door of the house shouting "Daaaaaddy!". Five years later and I can happily say that my dream has come true. How did I achieve it? I try to make each of my children feel that they are truly valued. I know they are, and I know that you know your children are, but do you really make them feel this way? To achieve this, I follow a very simple method. I look at them as if they were an actual piece of treasure. I smile at them. I spend as much time as I can with them. I include them in my plans so they know it is a privilege to be with them. I allow them to see how much I love them, and I tell them how much I love who they are. And my secret weapon: every time I enter the house, I throw my coat down, I kneel on the floor and I cry out for them enthusiastically. They come running to say hello and give me back the same love that I am giving them. Don't expect your children to adore you if you don't first make them feel that they are special every day of their lives. The secret of having the relationship you have always dreamt of with your children is simply to build it with them on a daily basis.

Remember

A positive and secure bond is necessary for the child's brain development. Self-confidence and the world in which they live are the foundations of good emotional intelligence. To achieve this, hug them and kiss them often, spend quality time with them and talk to them in a reciprocal way, avoid betraying their confidence and make them feel like they are exceptional and valued.

15

Confidence

> All you need in this life is ignorance and confidence; then success is sure.
> (Mark Twain)

Possibly one of the greatest gifts you can give your child is confidence. There is nothing that makes a person go further than feeling capable of achieving what they have set about doing. As Roosevelt said: "Believe you can and you're halfway there". In the previous chapter we talked about how a great bond can help the child develop love for themselves. The other side of self-esteem is confidence. It is difficult to build good self-esteem if it is not complemented by a good dose of confidence.

The child who grows up with confidence becomes an adult who feels good about themselves and others, who is sure of the decisions they make, who can laugh out loud, who feels an inner strength that makes them believe they can reach any life goal. I am sure there is not one mother, father or teacher who does not want their children or students to develop wonderful self-confidence and feel able to make their dreams come true. However, sometimes it is the educators themselves who sow doubt in the child's brain. In this chapter we are going to look at attitudes that can strengthen the child's confidence and those that stand in the way of their full development.

We know that confidence has a genetic component. There is a gene on chromosome 17 that predisposes each of us to have a greater or lesser degree of confidence. There are self-assured children and there are others who are shy. There are children who at just three years of age are able to ask a distant relative for a sip of their Coca-Cola, and others who hide from their favourite uncle aged five. There are those who are boldly able to say "no", and those who are silent in their opinions. There is also the five-year-old child who can organise a whole football team and the one who does not dare put up their hand to be selected. All that said, any child can gain confidence when the conditions are right for them. When the one who organised the football team disappears, another one always takes their place. When the older brother disappears, the little one becomes more determined and

DOI: 10.4324/9781003360117-19

responsible. Likewise, when the mother is absent or their peers of the same age disappear and the younger children appear, all children gain security. This tells us that all children have the ability to have a high level of self-confidence. They only need the right conditions; feeling the responsibility and confidence of those around them.

Depriving the child of their confidence

Needless to say, there is no obligation to take a child to nursery; in fact, there are many parents who do not. Although I must also say that as far as I know, there is no statistic that speaks of the number of children that do not get past that first day of nursery. If you do decide to take your child, ideally you should be able to join them on their first day or on a visit, so they can explore the classroom for a time while you are there talking with their teachers (without them noticing that you are aware of everything they do). The child must feel that you trust them so much that you don't even have to pay attention to them as they are in a safe place. Not all nursery schools have an adaptation process with so many guarantees, although I must add that this strategy does not guarantee a good adaptation. Today almost all schools try to do it in a progressive way, limiting the first periods of separation to one or two hours. One after another, all children adapt progressively and securely to their new surroundings. Something that helps them is to feel that their parents are calm and not showing signs of terror, or tears on their faces. The truth is that this first separation is a difficult moment for almost everyone who has children (and for almost all children). However, an attitude of calm and confidence when leaving them and a big smile and open arms when picking them up will help the child to adapt to the new situation as quickly as possible. Without a doubt, one of the things that most harms the child's confidence is too much fussing and over-protectiveness. I know it can be difficult not to intervene when we see that our child is about to take a tumble, or when we feel that they are facing a situation in which they could do with a little help. However, it is in these situations that their brain needs more of our trust. When a child faces a challenge, a situation that may not turn out well, their brain prepares itself to cope with it.

There are two main protagonists in the brain when it comes to confidence. Firstly, there is the "amygdala". This structure is one of the most important parts of the emotional brain. It works as an alarm that is activated every time the brain detects a dangerous situation. Secondly, the frontal lobe in the rational brain exerts a control function, offering the child the possibility of mastering fear and keeping going. If you remember our lesson on limits, you will know that somehow the frontal lobe is able to put limits on fear. Well, whenever there is a situation with a certain level of danger, these two parts of the brain fight against each other to see which is stronger. If the

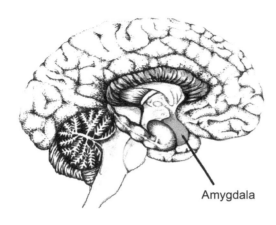

Amygdala
- Identify threats
- Activate the alarm signal
- Feel fear
- Memory of fear

Amygdala

amygdala wins, the child will get a fright. If the frontal lobe wins, fear will be under control.

Let's suppose that a child who has been walking for a few months, is struggling to get onto a park bench. In this scenario, there are three possible situations: (1) the parent does not intervene, (2) the parent intervenes calmly and (3) the parent intervenes in a state of panic. If the child's parent is calm, the child's brain will remain alert, even if they fall over or feel slightly anxious. If the parents intervene, they will be taking away the protagonist of the child's determination. The emotional brain will not feel calm because the child is not in control of it; they will learn that they need their parent to feel good. If the mother lets off a scream, the dad runs over, or the child detects an expression of horror on his or her parents' faces, their brain will release an alarm signal. In this case, the amygdala will be activated and the child will immediately feel terror.

I'm scared, but I'm in control of it.	My brain knows that it can control the fear.
I'm scared, but I'm not in control of it. My parents always help me.	Only my parents can control my fear.
I'm scared and my parents are in a state of panic.	I have to be afraid because the world is dangerous.

In this sense, regardless of where the child starts from, their confidence depends directly on the confidence their parents give them. If the parents spend all day worried about their health, safety or wellbeing, the child's brain is only able to understand two things: that the world is dangerous and that they are not at all capable of facing life by themselves. In the face of any challenge or new situation, the child will receive an alarm signal in their amygdala that will make them react with fear, avoid the challenge and hide behind their mother's skirt. However, those children whose parents place more confidence in them will be able to activate the coping mechanisms and keep them activated, even in the face of uncertainty.

I usually offer parents a formula to help them remember the importance of having confidence in their child when he or she is developing their own confidence.

$$CN = (PCoC)^2$$

The child's confidence is equal to the square of the parents' confidence in the child.

There is an old story about confidence in which two brothers, aged seven and five, were caught in a fire at a time when their mother had gone out of the house. They did not realise the danger until the flames had reached the door of their bedroom. Somehow, they managed to unlock the window, unhook the heavy emergency ladder and lower themselves down onto the safety of the street. When the neighbours and other people asked how two small children had managed to perform such a feat, the fire officer did not hesitate in his reply: "They did it because there was no adult there to tell them that they wouldn't be able to it on their own".

I know that sometimes acting on trust is difficult. Often from the point of view of the parents, the child is a dependent being and must be protected. Personally, I find it to be the most difficult part of my job as a father. Whenever I have doubts about it, I use my first principle and wait to see what happens. There was a time, at the beginning of last summer, when I noticed that my older children had lost confidence, especially when they were in the park surrounded by other children. My wife and I spoke about it; I thought about nothing else for a couple of days. Again and again, the principle that every child is like a tree, destined to develop themselves fully, came to my mind. All of a sudden, I understood that what they needed from us was a little more confidence. I talked to my wife, and although she took a protective stance – and I was afraid I was going to have to sleep on the couch for the rest of the week – we carried out a little experiment in the park. Usually we go up to them several times in the park, putting on and taking off their jumpers, asking them to stay away from certain places, or to play with them. That day we decided to spend the afternoon in the park without making any comments at all. It was wonderful! The children came and went, they asked for their jumpers when they were cold, and water when they were thirsty, they dared to climb where they would normally be afraid to go, and they made a group of friends of all ages running around and playing with them. I can't remember a time when I had seen them having so much fun with other children. I have been able to prove time and time again how trusting my child, keeping still and watching them provides a wonderful scene in which my child can almost always develop complete confidence. That summer we learnt a very important lesson: as far as confidence is concerned, less is more. Here you can see a table with some of the situations where it is better for you to let your child act freely and where the intervention of the parents is necessary.

Situations where it is not appropriate to protect the child	Situations where we must protect the child
• When they are happily playing on their own. • When they are playing with other children. • When they are interacting with other adults. • When they have taken a decision about something (even though it could be improved on). • Risk of a minor bump or fall. • Risk of a scratch or fright.	• Danger of injury or accident. • Danger of death. • Danger of intoxication. • Physically aggressive behaviour. • Situations of abuse.

Offer positive messages

Another effective strategy to build confidence in your child is to offer them positive messages. As we saw in the tools section, the negative messages ("You are lazy", "You are doing it wrong") do not help the child to do things better – they may actually cause anxiety and undermine their self-esteem. Instead, give your child positive messages when they overcome something. They may be doing something really difficult, concentrating hard, making an effort, showing courage or simply doing something which they weren't able to last summer. Offering messages like "You've been very brave", "You've been concentrating really hard", will help them have confidence in themselves. In this sense, it is important to know that rather than rewarding the result, the main thing is to recognise the child's attitude in doing it. We know that when a child is recognised for the result (for example, "You've done this jigsaw so well"), the neurons responsible for receiving rewards will look for other tasks that they can perform well. This is because they have learnt that the reward comes when the task is done well. Thus, when the result is not what they expected, the child tends to avoid complex tasks or ones that carry the risk of failure. They become frustrated disproportionately and may even avoid difficult tasks at all costs. When the child recognises other more interesting variables from the point of view of what is happening inside their brain, such as how hard they have concentrated, how clever they have been in solving a problem, how much they have enjoyed doing it or the effort they have put in for example, the child will then look for harder tasks, which allow him or her to keep striving, overcoming hurdles and enjoying their ability to think, concentrate and solve problems.

Up until the end of the 1970s it was thought that the best way to motivate a child was to praise their effort. There are many studies that have tried to find the most effective phrase or message to boost a child's motivation and confidence. Nowadays we know that there is no perfect formula, because at each moment every child uses a certain ability to get what they want. The key is always to emphasise the skill that the child puts into practice and to support them when they use tools that they don't normally use. In order to do this, you just have to pay attention when they are fulfilling tasks and ask yourself simple questions. How did she get that little box open? Was it perseverance? Ingenuity? How did he do that drawing? Was he meticulous? Concentrating hard? Did he make sure that he did not go outside the lines? Did he enjoy it? It is not even necessary for you to put too much effort into reinforcement or to make a big fuss, because their brain already knows how they did it and they already feel the satisfaction of having achieved it. Perhaps it is not enough to reward only the result; the effort, concentration or perseverance that went into it should also be valued when they show it.

Responsibility

Responsibility is an unavoidable part of existence. As much as life may appear to be something beautiful and wonderful, nature also teaches us that there is a harsher, fiercer side to life; that of the struggle for one's own subsistence. There is no living being who does not have to fight for or find their own food or shelter to survive. I often find myself in consultation with adults who suffer distress over the small responsibilities of everyday life. Working, cooking, paying bills or taking care of their children is simply too hard. In these cases, I wonder to what extent these people have been educated in being responsible for the large and small tasks of life. To many people, the word "responsibility" sounds severe. Sometimes I have been asked in my lectures if it is not too difficult for a two-year-old child to have responsibilities. I really don't think so. From my point of view, responsibility is nothing more than caring for yourself; educating others in responsibility is a great opportunity to teach children to take care of themselves and to know how to assert themselves.

Responsibility is an excellent way to develop a child's confidence. Every child can take responsibility for many tasks in their education and care. The sooner they start doing them, the easier they will seem and the more confidence they will acquire in their own abilities. The most interesting thing is that children love responsibilities. For them it is an opportunity to discover new things and to be in control of their environment. You can start from the moment the child starts to walk. As they do at school, children can – and, from my point of view, should – help to clear away their toys, and can also throw their nappies in the bin. I live very close to our nursery, so my three children have walked there since they were one year old. The three minutes it took to cross the two streets that separate us from the nursery became fifteen or twenty at a baby's pace. To date, no one has complained, partly because at twelve or thirteen months of age children cannot speak, but also because they enjoyed their morning walk. Once they arrive at their classroom, they have always been the first to go in. I have helped them, I have encouraged them and I have held their hand, but they have always been the ones to set foot inside their classroom, simply because it is not my job to put them in their classroom; it is their job to go inside. These are just examples for you to see that responsibility is something that can be introduced from a very young age through small gestures. As they grow up, you can teach them how to throw dirty clothes into the basket, clear away their cup when they have finished breakfast, or clean something when it gets dirty – the spilt milk on the table, for example. It is not a punishment if you treat it as a natural fact that the child takes care of themselves and their own things – alone or with a little help. At every age there is a series of tasks that the child can take on to help them feel confident, all the while learning to participate in domestic chores. I assure you that they will love to take care of their own duties and will grow up feeling satisfied and able to take care of themselves.

Validate their feelings and decisions

We have already seen the importance of empathy for a child to be able to understand that all their feelings are important and valuable. Knowing that we can be angry, happy or frustrated in different situations – while respecting the rights of others – is a good source of self-confidence. Another important area in the development of confidence, and where parents sometimes slip up, is in decision making. It is common for mothers and fathers to insist on helping their children make better decisions. A typical example may be the following: "Paula, what do you want for your birthday?" "A packet of strawberry flavoured chewing gum, mummy", "But Paula, that's not much, you can ask for something bigger if you like!". Different versions of this simple conversation are repeated every year around the same date, and the result is always the same. The little girl, excited over a packet of chewing gum, ends up asking for a doll that she couldn't care less about.

Many people feel insecure when making decisions. They don't know what clothes to wear, they are indecisive about what to order in a restaurant, they are not sure if they should say this or that, and they end up being the protagonist in their soap opera of doubts, indecisions and dilemmas. One part of their brain is always clear about what they want, while there is another that makes them doubt. In this sense, the brain is like a discussion between the rational and the emotional brain. Doubt almost never begins on the side of emotion; it usually appears from the side of reason. In actual fact, we know that the vast majority of decisions – whether ordering a dish in a restaurant, choosing your partner, or buying a house – are made by the emotional brain. In most cases, the rational brain is only responsible for justifying the choice or providing a logical reason to explain the decision we make in a visceral way. It has also been proven that the best decisions usually come from the emotional brain rather than the rational one. It has also been shown that those who weigh up alternatives from a more rational point of view tend to be more insecure and make worse decisions. Even if it may seem otherwise, a good way to help your child make better decisions is to allow them to make decisions guided by their instinct and to trust them to learn from their own mistakes. Of course they will make mistakes, who doesn't? Far from preventing each mistake from happening, a good strategy is to teach the child to trust themselves and help them to learn the positive and negative lessons from them.

Remember

Confidence is one of the best gifts we can give to our children. A child who grows up feeling that their parents have confidence in them will grow to be an adult who is capable of achieving their goals and aspirations. Avoid overprotecting your child; trust them and their ability to develop fully.

Offer them responsibilities and support them in both their emotions and their decisions. Don't forget that when you want to boost their confidence, the smartest strategy is not only placing value on the results, but acknowledging their effort, level of concentration or enjoyment when dealing with a difficult situation.

16

Growing up without fear

Modern science has not yet produced a calming medicine as effective as a few kind words.

(Sigmund Freud)

An essential part of the development of emotional intelligence is being able to overcome our own fears. As with all of us, during their childhood your child will experience situations that cause fear. Being bitten by a dog, shoved by a friend or simply falling from a certain height can impact deeply on their brain and cause disproportionate fear when faced with similar situations. Knowing how to handle these situations will allow you to help your child deal with fear during childhood, but most importantly, it can help them to live a life free from fear, as the way in which a child learns to face their fears from a young age will determine the way they do it when he or she is an adult.

Many parents do not know what to do when their child encounters a traumatic experience. Some parents become agitated and shout at the child, causing a higher degree of alarm in the brain and increasing the trauma. In other cases, the natural response of the parent is to ask the child to calm down and to downplay the situation. Believe it or not, this attitude can be as harmful as the previous one. Certainly, making light of the situation when a child has tripped or has been frightened by something will lighten the emotional load and help the child to calm down. However, when the fright is more serious and the child's brain is not able to overcome the situation on their own, fear can take a hold of them. I will now explain two very simple strategies to help your child to overcome these traumas, and above all teach them to successfully face up to any fear that comes their way.

Help them to assimilate traumatic experiences

If you think back to what I showed you in Chapter 4 (the top three things to know of the brain) you will remember that there are two hemispheres.

DOI: 10.4324/9781003360117-20

The left is more rational, and the right is more intuitive; and it is in the right hemisphere where traumatic scenes are recorded. If you are able to remember any traumatic experience from your life, you will know that some of those scenes are remembered in the form of images. Soldiers returning home from war experience flashbacks, which are nothing more than flashes of images that the brain is not able to process. In most cases, fears grow in the right part of the brain, and live in the more intuitive and visual hemisphere in the form of images and sensations. When the traumatic experience is minor, the child is able to understand it for themselves. For example, they are able to understand that a doll has broken because it fell to the floor. However, if the fright is more serious, the child may not be able to process the experience and then what we know as "irrational fear" appears. As an example, suppose a dog runs over to your son, barking. Although the dog's owner is able to stop it in time, your child's brain has two very clear images. First, the image of the dog attacking him, and secondly, the feeling of panic. These images are so strong that if we do nothing to prevent them, they can remain etched on his brain forever and the child can develop an irrational fear of dogs. You can dilute these images and deactivate the traumatic images from their brain. All you have to do is help your child talk about what he has seen and what he has felt. When a frightened person speaks and describes what happened, their left hemisphere (the one in charge of speaking) begins to communicate with the right hemisphere. In this simple way, you will be helping the verbal and logical part of the brain to help the visual and emotional part to overcome the experience. We call this process "integrating the traumatic experience". The child will remember the event, but will no longer experience it with the same level of anxiety. They will have integrated it with normality as an unpleasant experience of their past. In Figure 16.1 you can see a representation of how the process works.

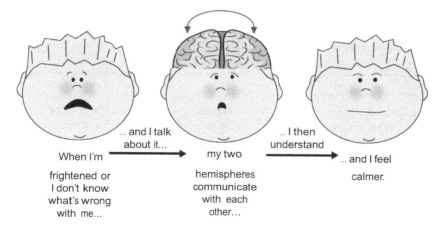

When I'm frightened or I don't know what's wrong with me... ... and I talk about it... my two hemispheres communicate with each other... ... I then understand ... and I feel calmer.

Talking to a child about a traumatic situation requires calm – you might be as scared as they are – peace – it may take a long time to calm down – a little faith – since this action can go against your impulse to reassure the child – and a great deal of empathy – as we saw in the tools section. It is natural that your first reaction is to downplay it. After all, if you manage to convince the child that they are not afraid, you will also be calmer. However, the important thing is not to convince either of you that the scare was nothing, but to convince their brain they can move past it. Let's see an example: little Clare leaves school crying. An older boy took her toy and pushed her to the ground. Obviously, you need to talk to the school so that this does not happen again, but in the meantime, how do we deal with Clare's fright? Here are two very different approaches.

Play down its importance	Help her to integrate it
M: Why are you crying, Clare?	M: Why are you crying, Clare?
C: An older boy hit me.	C: An older boy hit me.
M: That's ok, darling ...	M: And did you get a fright?
C: He pushed me over.	C: Yes.
M: It's ok, it doesn't matter, you'll get over it.	M: Of course you did, he's bigger than you are.
C: (Still crying).	C: (Still crying).
M: It's ok, calm down.	M: And what did he do to you?
C: (Still crying).	C: He pushed me over.
M: Come on, Clare. You're a big girl!	M: Did he push you hard?
C: (Sobbing).	C: (Her tears begin to dry). Yes. Like this, with his hand.
M: You're a brave girl! And brave girls don't cry.	M: He pushed you really hard with his hand?
C: (She goes quiet and looks at the floor).	C: Yes. (She's no longer crying.)
M: Well done! See what a big girl you are? Come on, let's go home and I'll make you a milkshake.	M: I'm not surprised you were scared. I would be too. Did he give you a horrible look?
	C: Yes, he looked angry. He's horrible.
	M: Yes, he gave you a big fright, didn't he?
	C: Yes.
	M: You're feeling a bit better now aren't you? I'm going to speak to your teacher so this boy doesn't hit you again.
	C. I'm going to play.

The first example is the typical conversation that we can observe between parents and children in the park. Here the mother tries play down the situation and approaches the little girl, telling her she is brave and that she must calm down. In the second example, the mother talks for a while about specific aspects of the incident and analyses the images and sensations that are trapped in the right hemisphere of the child's brain. She asks specifically what the other child did, stops to see how big he is, as well as his facial expressions. At different times, it also emphasises how scared the girl felt. In these responses we can see that the little girl gradually begins to feel calmer. As you can see, the second technique requires a little more time and conversation than the first, but without a doubt it is the safest way for the brain to feel safe and calm.

Let's look at another example. Adam has just watched a scene from a scary film at his uncle John's house. In the scene, a person is being chased by a zombie while stretching out their arms to grab the person. That night, when Adam returns home, his uncle John tells you that the boy was very frightened. He assures you that he tried to calm him down, but he was very scared. That night you decide to talk to your child before he goes to sleep. Let's look at the difference between the uncle's way of dealing with the situation, and that of a father who knows how to help their son integrate a traumatic experience.

Uncle John	Dad
A: (Crying). UJ: Come on Adam, don't be scared. A: (Still crying). UJ: But zombies aren't real! A: (Still crying). UJ: Zombies don't do anything! A: (Adam buries his head in a cushion). UJ: Look, Adam, it's just a stupid zombie, it can't hurt you. A: (Continues to bury his head and cry). UJ: Look! I'm a zombie! Raaahhh!! A: I don't want to look! UJ: It's just a joke! A: It's not funny! I want to see my mum! UJ: Ok, we can see your mum, but only when you calm down. If not, you're going to scare her. A: (Adam calms down, with a frightened look on his face).	D: Uncle John told me that you got a fright? A: Yes, there was a zombie. D: And did it give you a fright? A: Yes. (Begins to cry). D: Of course, zombies are really scary. A: Yes. D: And what did it do to make you so scared? A: (Sobbing). It was chasing a man. D: Wow, that must have scared you a lot. A: Yes, he was trying to grab him. D: And what did you do? A: I closed my eyes. (He is no longer crying). D: Of course, you didn't want to watch. A: Yes, because it was so scary. D: And what did it look like? A: He was covered in blood and held his arms out like this. D: And what else? A: And it opened his mouth like this. It was a really silly zombie. (He laughs). D: I think you feel a bit calmer now. Tomorrow we can speak about it again. Ok? It's time for bed my little champion!

It is important to show warmth and be close by when talking to the child about events that have caused them fear. The child must feel very close to you and believe that you understand them perfectly, otherwise they will feel that we are laughing at them. There is no need to be dramatic, just be calm and listen with empathy, try to understand how the child felt at the time. It is also very important to review the story two or three times over the next few days. The more the child processes the images and impressions verbally, the more the event will be integrated. I can assure you that when a young child is sad or scared there is nothing that helps them more than talking about it with a person who understands it perfectly. In fact, the same thing happens to adults! Help your child process traumatic experiences with both brain hemispheres and they will into grow self-confident, fearless adults.

Help the child face up to their fears

Fears are a natural part of the child's development. As much as you try to prevent your child from having "traumatic" experiences, or help them to integrate them as I have taught you, there will always be a certain fear that will get to them in one way or another. When this happens, there is a strategy that can help the child to overcome their childhood fears, as well as learning to overcome any fear that they experience throughout their life. The strategy is none other than helping them to face their fears.

There are two emotions that can only be overcome by facing them. The first is fear, and the second is shame. They are practically the same. If you have ever fallen off your bike you will know that the only one way to overcome your fear is to get back on. There are two types of fear: instinctive and acquired. Instinctive fears are those that appear in the child naturally, without any previous experience that has caused them. Most people have a natural fear of snakes. In the same way, many children may experience fear touching a dog, getting into a swimming pool, or being in the dark. Acquired fears appear when a previous experience determines that we feel fear in a similar situation. If the child falls from a tree, they may become afraid of heights, and if an older child threw sand at another child in the park, they may develop fear of approaching unknown children.

When faced with a frightened child, a parent may want to console the child by hugging them, showing empathy and making the child feel that their parent will protect them from all evil. Although it is essential that the child feels safe and protected, and every parent will do well to show their child that they are in a safe environment, what is not so effective is to feel satisfied that this momentary protection is enough. Although parents and many children would like it, the reality is that it is impossible for one always to protect the child. Often parents adopt a strategy of greater confrontation, encouraging the child to face their fears at the same time, without realising that they can feel like a lamb to the slaughter. In the first case the child may experience lack of confidence and great a tendency to avoid difficult situations or those that require a certain degree of courage. The second case may turn out well, but the child's fear is frequently exacerbated, so this macho approach is also not recommended. As with so many other things, the middle ground, a balance, actually seems to be a much more effective strategy.

Without a doubt, it is worth helping the child to overcome their fears. For this, I would advise dealing with it in seven stages, which go from fear to trust, and use many of the tools that I gave you in the first chapters. We will use a practical example to complement the explanation of these seven steps that will help you understand and remember the technique. Sonia is four years old. She loves to balance along things and climb up high. One day she walks along a plank positioned at a certain height, and somehow loses her concentration and falls. The height was not excessive – if not, you would not have let her go up there – but you notice on her face that she had a big scare and says, very nervously, that she will not climb up high again. Let's see how Sonia can overcome this "acquired" fear with her mother's help.

1. Use empathy to calm the emotional brain that only feels the need to run away. It may take a little time.	M: (Taking her in her arms). What a fright you had! S: (Crying). Yes!! M: Of course, you fell off and it gave you a big fright. S: (Crying less). Yes!! (The mother continues to use empathy until the child calms down)
2. Validate the fear and speak about the importance of facing up to this fear.	M: I know, you've told me you don't want to get back up there, right? S: Yes. M: Of course, but it's important that we try again, so that you aren't frightened. S: I don't want to.
3. Use cooperative communication so that she knows that you're going to get over this fear together.	M: I know, I can imagine. Let's try and do it together. S: I'm scared. M: Mummy's going to help you. We'll do it together and I'll hold your hand.
4. Try to reach an agreement about what you both want to achieve.	M: Let's try doing it together, but only going a little way up. S: But I'm scared. M: Let's try something. You only have to take two steps, and I'll be holding your hand. What do you think?
5. Do it only when the child is ready, without pressure and without forcing them.	S: OK, but you take my hand. M: I'm not going to let you go. Take my hand. Come on, you take the first step.
6. Ask the child how satisfied or happy they feel and value their ability to overcome their fear.	M: Well done!! You did that on your own! I only gave you my hand. How do you feel? S: Yes I've been very brave! M: Yes, you look very pleased with yourself. S: Yes, I want to try going a bit further.
7. Do the same thing again, on a different day in another context, to enable the child to generalise the situation.	

It is very important to keep in mind that these seven steps take time. However, what are a few minutes in exchange for a life without fear? Helping the child to calm down is the step that takes more time. However, those three or four minutes invested in connecting with their emotional brain are key to being able to open the door of courage. You should also keep in mind that, as shown in step 5, an important point is not to force the child at any time. We must not push them or drag them. We can take their hand to be with them, but it must be the child who takes the first step, or at least the one who lets themselves be gently guided. The opposite will only provoke an escape response, that which we are helping the child to take control of.

Remember

Helping a child to prevent and overcome their fears is an easy task for parents if they know how. To accomplish this you just need to spend a little time talking to the child and being both respectful and understanding of their feelings, the time they need to be able to calm down, and the amount of help they need to face their fear and to feel courage. It is a natural instinct to accompany and protect a child who is experiencing fear, but remember that you can choose to be their partner for running away, or their partner in courage.

Scientific studies and common sense tell us that the second option is what can teach your child to overcome any fear they have in their life.

Assertiveness

Don't worry that your children never listen to you … they are always watching.

(Mother Teresa of Calcutta)

A common characteristic of people with good emotional intelligence is that they are assertive. The term "assertiveness" refers to the person's ability to say what they are thinking in a respectful way. An assertive person is able to express both what he or she does not want or like, and also what they do want or like, in a way that is as clear as it is respectful.

Assertiveness is a way of communicating with others in order to feel confident in our rights, our opinions and our feelings, and that we can express them to another person in a respectful manner. Without a doubt, an important part of the job of any parent or teacher who wants to help their children feel good about themselves and achieve their goals is to teach them to be assertive. All experts agree that assertiveness offers great advantages to those who apply it. They feel more sure of themselves, they lessen the risk of conflicts with others and they are more effective in reaching their goals.

Assertiveness is most noticeable in people who have high levels of confidence. Likewise, any person taught to communicate in an assertive way gains confidence in themselves and in their relationships with others. This is because assertive people experience lower levels of anxiety and their brain secretes less cortisol, the stress hormone. Interestingly, when an anxious

DOI: 10.4324/9781003360117-21

person has a conversation with an assertive person, they feel relaxed and their cortisol levels are reduced. Therefore, assertive people are often born leaders. Another relevant point that you should know about assertiveness, and on which all experts agree, is that the sooner assertiveness is implemented into the child's education, the more self-confidence they will have. I will now give you three key points with which to help you to teach your child to be assertive in their communication

Be assertive

If you remember the chapter in which we talked about how you can motivate a child's behaviour, the starting point was simply to provide examples that the child could copy. Thanks to the mirror neurons, the child's brain practises and learns the repertoire of behaviour it observes in its parents. In the case of assertiveness, the observation of assertive behaviour in parents appears to be a decisive factor. If the child observes their parent confront small interpersonal conflicts with clarity and respect, they will develop an assertive communication style. Some parents are not very assertive with other people. They may have a tendency to show aggressiveness and/or passivity. If you belong to this first group, your natural tendency is to go after what you want, to value your own rights over those of your neighbour and to communicate in a coarse and forceful way during conflicts. If you are from the second group, your personal style makes you avoid conflict. You will keep quiet or express your opinions timidly without asserting your rights. In either case, it is important that you know that your children are watching you. When they find themselves in a conflict, they will most likely imitate you, just as they would imitate their older sibling who says a swear word. In this sense, it would be helpful to remember that your child will take you as a model of behaviour in the face of conflict; so you can decide whether acting in an aggressive manner, or keeping quiet in the face of abuse is what you really want to show your child.

I don't want you to picture this as something from a Hollywood film. Assertiveness is learnt through small gestures and conversations with parents that arise in the day-to-day life of their children. Another parent may suggest that you go to the park together and you don't feel like it. It may be that a child unintentionally takes your child's toy, or that someone stands in front of you in the supermarket queue. In these cases, remember that your child is watching you. Are you going to act with excessive force or disrespect? Are you going to keep quiet and accept things as they are? Or are you going to express what you mean with freedom and confidence? I advise you to keep this chapter in mind and try to bring out your assertive side. Comment, express yourself and do what you really want to do, without fear and without anger, openly and respectfully.

Be assertive in day-to-day situations.

Instead of ...	Try ...
Going with the other parent to the park when you don't feel like it.	"Thanks, but I don't fancy the park today."
Allowing the child to take the toy.	"Hello, little one, I think that toy is ours."
Shouting at the man who has jumped the queue at the supermarket.	"Excuse me, but we were first in the queue."

Although it is important to be assertive with friends and strangers, the main issue in showing our children our assertive side is at home. The biggest obstacle in helping the child to be assertive, is that many parents are not assertive enough with their children. We can create a range of excuses, tell fibs and make a fuss in order to avoid having to deal with our children being angry: "Sweetheart, the shop has run out of lollipops", "The man says you're not allowed to run in the supermarket, darling", "We are going to another park because the one you want to go to is closed". To be honest, we have made great advancements if we compare this to years ago, when the bogeyman or the monsters would come and take away children who misbehaved. But there are still many of us who are not entirely open and honest with our children. Take for example, a couple dealing with a four-year-old son who was hooked on video games, using their tablet and smartphone. To overcome this, the parents told the child that the internet had stopped working, meaning that he wouldn't be able to use the mobile phone or tablet. For two months they had not looked at their mobile phones in front of the boy so he wouldn't know it was a lie. Assertiveness requires a little more honesty and courage.

When we tell a child a fib, they learn to tell them too. Furthermore, they learn that they have to hide certain things, they cannot trust their own judgement, and they should avoid speaking openly. Assertive people do not tell lies, they express their opinions and decisions as and when they feel them. They use expressions like "I want", "I feel like it", "I feel", "I think", "I don't want", or "I don't feel like it". It is certainly true that confronting the child's desire openly, telling him or her: "I don't want you to eat sweets", is a little harder than convincing them with some falsehood. It may be that the first few times the child becomes angry and has a tantrum – especially if you are not used to setting limits clearly; however, if you act assertively with the child, without fibbing or being deceitful, you will triumph in two invaluable ways. Firstly, you will have taught the child to be assertive. Secondly, and perhaps more importantly, you will have forever earned your child's respect. I cannot imagine a more valuable educational tool than a child feeling respect for their parents or teachers. Respect will allow your child to be guided by you, respect you and put all their trust in you. Not only will it help you to educate them, but they will be able to contribute in a very decisive way so that you can build and maintain a good relationship with them.

Try being more assertive in your relationship with your child.

Instead of saying ...	Try ...
"It's not allowed."	"I don't want you to."
"There are no sweets left."	"I don't want you to eat sweets right now."
"You have to eat everything."	"I want you to finish everything."
"The internet doesn't work."	"I don't want you to go on the
"Daddy can't play right now."	internet."
"The man says that you are not allowed to run."	"I don't feel like it right now, sweetheart."
	"I don't want you to run in here."

Respect and assert their rights

All programmes that are designed to develop assertiveness make clear the importance of the participant making their rights known as individuals. Unassertive people react aggressively for fear of being trampled on by others, or with resignation because they do not feel sure about what they can and cannot ask for. In both cases, knowing our fundamental rights as people helps us to feel confident about what we can say, feel and think, and assert our opinions towards other people. If you assert them and help your children to grow up knowing them and feeling that each of these rights deserves to be respected, you will have contributed to the child feeling good about themselves throughout their childhood, and later on as an adult, in an incalculable way.

The following are the fundamental rights I keep in my home and firmly believe that we should all transmit to our children in the home.

The right to be treated with respect and dignity

Do not disrespect your children or let anyone else do it, otherwise their brain will learn that they are not worthy of respect.

The right to have and express their own feelings and opinions

Listen to their opinions with genuine attention and interest. You don't have to always do what they say, but it is important that you always give their opinions the same respect and consideration that you want your child to feel for themselves.

The right to be able to determine their own needs, establish their priorities and make their own decisions

Pay attention to their gestures and their words. Your child knows what story they want you to read them, when they are full and do not want to eat more, or when they don't want to take part in the plan that you suggest. Let the child decide for him or herself, provided you have the choice.

The right to say "no" without feeling guilty

We can all have our own opinion, refuse to do something, and not feel guilty about it. If your child does not want to have a bath on a specific day, assess whether it is something that can be overlooked. Let them make the decision or set the limit, but don't make them feel guilty about it as they will grow up feeling guilt and anger every time they get their own way.

The right to ask for what they want

We all have the right to ask for what we want, as long as we understand that the other person is also free to agree to our wishes or not.

The right to change

Each person has the right to change their mind, their tastes, their interests or their hobbies. Respect your child's right to choose something that is different to what they had initially chosen.

The right to decide what they want to do with their own belongings and body, while respecting the rights of others

Your child may decide to exchange one of their toys with a friend or to draw on their own foot with a marker pen. We have to educate our children, and we will not allow them to do something that harms or endangers them. But what is wrong with swapping toys if both children agree to it, or drawing a dinosaur on the back of their leg? In my opinion, nothing at all.

The right to make a mistake

We all make mistakes. I make mistakes, you make mistakes and your child will of course make mistakes. Help them understand that it's ok when this happens.

The right to be successful

You might have felt worried because your son runs, jumps or reads well, while his brother or neighbour are not yet at that stage. Do not ignore or be ashamed of his qualities or achievements. We all have the right to succeed. The other children have their qualities as well. If you don't recognise those of your son, how do you think he himself will recognise them?

The right to rest and be alone

Similar to how you feel sometimes, a child may need to be alone, be in a quiet space or take a break, especially when they have been doing too much and are tired. They will see it as something normal, like drinking a glass of water when they are thirsty. Give them their space and allow them to be calm. After a short while they will most likely want to go and join their friends again.

This is the final one, and my favourite.

The right to not be assertive

Everyone can choose at a certain time if they want to be assertive. There are days when we feel less capable, we are with people who make us feel less strong or situations in which we are overcome with frustration and we react in a slightly more aggressive way than usual. It doesn't matter. Each situation and each person is different. Respect a child's right not to be assertive all the time. In some situations, passivity is the best tool for survival. Faced with an abusive situation, baring your teeth may be the only way out; and when a person is experiencing anxiety, knowing how to stay out of the way and not battling every little conflict is an intelligent emotional strategy. Being assertive in normal conditions is undoubtedly the best option, but in life not all situations or people are indeed normal. Do not limit your child's repertoire of communication and give them space so that that at different times they react in different ways. The child is young. Sometimes it is normal to be afraid. Respect their right not to always be assertive.

Give a voice to the silent one

The third key to helping your child be assertive is to give them a voice when they need to talk and can't. One of the first things that someone learns when they specialise in group therapy is to pay special attention to those members of the group who remain silent. When an emotionally complex subject is touched upon at a meeting, it is common for the member of the group who has the most to say to be the one who remains silent. The same can happen with children. I am going to share an experience with you that occurs in my family, that exemplifies the great importance of giving a voice to the silent one. A few months after the birth of our youngest daughter, my wife and I were really exhausted. Diego, our eldest son, had not yet turned four and his sisters of one and a half and two months were still very small. Both girls were waking up several times each night to breastfeed or be fed a bottle, and we were showing the signs of tiredness after having gone through three pregnancies, three births and raising three children in just four years. I remember that the crying began to bother me like never before, and for the first time in four years, I saw my wife lose her patience. In these circumstances it is normal for anyone to have their nerves frayed, and as usually happens, we argued more than usual. One Sunday morning we drove to see the children's grandparents and, without knowing how, my wife and I began to argue. I don't remember what we argued about. Possibly nothing in particular. What I do remember is that we reprimanded each other for things we had not done well, and we said some unpleasant things that related to the tension we both felt inside. We couldn't stop. Then I saw Diego in the rear-view mirror, sitting in his child seat, totally silent and staring at the floor. At that moment I knew that the situation was not fair for him. He wasn't enjoying it. I could have said: "Don't worry, Diego, parents are not going to argue anymore". However, I knew that I wasn't able to keep that promise, because all parents argue from time to time. Instead, I decided to give him a voice so that he could say what he really felt.

ME: How are you feeling, my love?
DIEGO: Not good.
ME: Because parents are arguing a lot, aren't they?
DIEGO: Yes. It makes me scared.
ME: You felt that you couldn't speak, is that right?
DIEGO: Right.
ME: So, Diego, what would you have liked to have said when you were so quiet?
DIEGO: (Very timidly). That I want you to stop arguing.
ME: Really? I think that's great. You should have said it. You should always say what you think. Especially if there is something that you don't like or that's bothering you. Hmm. Do you know that I think? I think you should say it to us, loudly. I'll help you.
DIEGO: Stop arguing.
ME: Louder!
DIEGO: Stop arguing!!!!
ME: Louder!!!!
DIEGO: STOP ARGUING!!!!

Diego was smiling and was happy again. I don't think I have ever felt prouder of my job as a father as the day I taught my eldest son to say what he thinks and to overcome his fear of saying it. As the months go by, my wife and I argue far less, but when we do, not once has Diego not told us to shut up or stop arguing. Sometimes we listen to him and sometimes we don't, but we always feel fine about it because not once have we seen him looking as sad as he did that day, sitting in his chair, not daring to speak. As parents, we can never be perfect. As Daniel Siegel and Tina Bryson say in their fantastic book *The Whole-Brain Child*, there are no "super parents". We all get angry, we argue and we are wrong, but if you teach your child to say what they think when they are being silent, you will be helping them to become a more assertive person, expressing what they feel and being able to ask for what they want. And you will know that they will be able to defend themselves even if the circumstances make them a little scared.

Remember

Assertiveness is a gift for any child. It will allow them to express their desires, fears and concerns freely. Starting from today, I encourage you to be a little more assertive with others, but especially with your child. Keep their rights in mind, respect them and assert them, giving them a voice when they feel weak or helpless. In this way the child learns to defend themselves and to always ask for what they want.

18

Sowing the seeds for happiness

If you want to be happy, be.

(Leo Tolstoy)

In the spring of 2000, I had the opportunity to attend a conference on childhood depression while doing my residency as a neuropsychologist in the United States. It was a unique opportunity to listen to a psychologist that all psychology students studied at the faculty. Dr Martin Seligman became famous in the late 1970s for developing a revolutionary theory about the origin of depression. On this occasion he spoke to us with great concern about the enormous increase in cases of childhood depression that at that time were being detected in the United States. According to this psychologist, the data was not only alarming, but according to their forecast, there would be an increase in cases in the years to come.

In his brilliant lecture, he explained how being able to tolerate frustration could help safeguard against depression. Furthermore, contrary to what seemed advisable, children were not exposed to frustrating situations in the same way as their parents or grandparents were. Although the internet boom had just begun, children were writing emails and chatting online at that time. Certain habits that cultivated the ability to resist frustration were being lost, such as waiting until the next day or until there was a reduced rate for talking to their classmates, or writing letters and waiting to receive them from friends in the summer holidays. According to Dr Seligman, if we did nothing to remedy the loss of parents' values, the model of instant gratification and the advancement of new technologies, it could have serious consequences on the mental health of our children. A few years later, all these predictions have come true. It is no longer necessary to sit in front of a computer to talk with friends, because all children have had technology and social networks in the palms of their hands even before reaching adolescence. Talking with a friend is as simple as looking up a football game or exploring the anatomy of the opposite

DOI: 10.4324/9781003360117-22

sex. You don't have to have the courage to talk to a romantic interest in person or put up with rejection, because the internet makes everything easier. There are children who don't talk in class, but chat when they get home, and parents are becoming increasingly complacent and permissive with their children.

Martin Seligman has become perhaps the most influential psychologist of our time. His concern for the advancement of depression led him to open a new field of research, and today he is known as the founder of "positive psychology", a branch of psychology focused on the search for the key to happiness. One of his main focuses of study is to understand what some people do to experience happiness and protect themselves from depression. After more than a decade of studies, we know many of the keys to happiness. The most interesting thing about positive psychology research is that all people can increase their levels of happiness by changing some of their habits and customs. You can help your children develop a positive thinking style by teaching them a few values and simple habits in your daily lives. Take out a pen and paper because what you are going to read next can help you and your children look at life with optimism.

ssLearn to tolerate frustration

A task that every child must learn throughout their life if they want to grow into a happy adult is to overcome frustration. Life is full of satisfying moments, both large and small, but also of frustrating moments, both large and small too. As we have already seen, no father can completely free his children from those moments of suffering or feelings of dissatisfaction, and therefore your child has no other choice than to learn how to cope with this frustration. Children have to understand that "no" is a common word, as they will hear it many times throughout their lives. You can help them understand it if you explain it to them, hold them in your arms or hug them when they are feeling overwhelmed and use empathy, but particularly if you can help them see that sometimes things just aren't meant to be. You may feel that this advice is lacking in depth and you would like to know more about how to help your child cope with frustration. In the chapter that addresses self-control, you can read more tricks and strategies to help you teach your child to take control of their frustration.

Avoid fulfilling all their wishes

There are many studies that show that there is no correlation between wealth and happiness. Although certain economic standards are necessary to avoid the suffering caused by hunger or the cold, it seems that once a particular level of security is reached, money does not lend itself to happiness. Studies show that happiness is not related to salary, social position or possessions. It is true that when we buy shoes or a new car, we feel satisfied, but this rush of happiness only seems to last a few minutes to a few days. Studies of lottery winners reveal that a few months after becoming millionaires, they were as happy or as unhappy as before their win. Avoiding fulfilling all your child's wishes will teach them three things that can help them to be happier in life. Firstly, happiness cannot be bought. Secondly, we cannot have everything we want in life, and thirdly, people feel happy because of how they are and how they relate to others.

Help them to practise patience

You can begin this from a very young age, when they need to be fed, or they feel discomfort for some reason. Instead of attending to them urgently, trust in their ability to wait. Do not become anxious when you hear their cries because you will only teach the child that frustration is a very distressing experience. Take care of their needs as soon as possible, but with the tranquillity and confidence of knowing that your baby can cope with a small amount of frustration. As the child grows, you can help them deal with frustration better by teaching them to respect limits, especially when it comes to time. It is good for their brain to learn that they must hold out at particular moments or wait their turn to get what they want. In this sense, you can teach them that before taking out a toy they must put away the one they are playing with, before eating they must wash their hands, before starting to paint they must clear the table and before being given that gift that will make them so happy, they will have to wait for their birthday, or another special occasion. They will certainly experience some frustration and impatience, but they will also learn to look forward to things, which is another characteristic of very happy people.

Focus their attention on the positive

There is no better way to be unhappy than to constantly think about the things you don't have. People who feel unhappy tend to focus their attention on what bothers or saddens them. Happy people, on the other hand, turn their attention to positive things. Fortunately, attention habits can be changed. Just as a dentist tends to notice people's smiles because their brain thinks as a dentist, you can help your child develop a positive attention style. A very simple strategy that you can apply when a child expresses frustration over what their friends have and what he or she does not have, is redirecting their attention onto all the material or immaterial things they are fortunate to be able to enjoy. It's not about rejecting their feelings, you can listen to the child with empathy, but at the same time you can help them think positively and explain that "people who focus on what they don't have, feel sad; people who focus on what they do have, feel happy and fortunate".

At home I put into practice a simple exercise that, through a positive psychology investigation, showed that people can be taught to direct their attention to the positives. For four weeks, some students wrote on paper each night three positive things that had happened to them throughout the day. After four weeks, their levels of happiness had increased significantly. Given the results of this interesting study, every night before reading a story, I ask my children to tell me two or three good things that happened that day. If you practise this simple exercise, you will not only help your children to focus their attention on the good side of things, you will also find out what things are really important to them. If I tell you the truth, thinking about the best things that have happened that day is not an activity that excites them very much, but their obstinate father makes it a necessary condition for reading them their bedtime story. I am convinced that this helps them to develop positive thinking, and if not, then putting up with their father at least helps them to exercise their patience.

Cultivate gratitude

Studies have shown that those who say "thank you" more often and those who feel more grateful reach higher levels of happiness. Part of the trick is that saying thank you helps to focus attention on the positive aspects of life. Say thank you and remind your child of the importance of being grateful to people. Whether you are religious or not, you can also take advantage of dinner time to thank or feel fortunate to have food on the table and to enjoy each other's company. This simple ritual will help children know how lucky they are and for all the things they have.

Help them enjoy activities which are rewarding

It may seem too simple an idea, but if you think about it, it is a powerful one. Those who spend time doing things they like are happier than those who spend more time doing things they don't like. Specifically, it has been shown that people who have hobbies and are able to immerse themselves in an activity such as painting, sport or cooking, to the point of losing track of time, are happier than those who do not. Respect and encourage the moments in which your child is entertaining themselves, drawing, arranging their dolls, building things or looking at stories, because the ability to detach themselves and lose track of time is very valuable from the point of view of happiness.

Sowing the seeds
for happiness

Cultivating patience

Gratitude

Acknowledging
achievements and
capabilities

Overcoming fears

Acceptance

Bonds

Tolerating frustration

Thinking positively

Time for exploring

Empathy

Confidence

Security

In the same way, you can also help the child to get away from things they don't like or that make them feel bad. Sometimes children become obsessed with a friend who is not kind to them. You can encourage them to play with children who they enjoying being with, without feeling bad. Help them to understand that playing with that child who treats them badly does not make them feel good. Knowing how to choose friendships is also key to emotional wellbeing.

Remember

Happiness is a combination of character, security, confidence. It is the ability to assert our rights and it is about having a positive outlook on life. You can help your child build a positive thinking style by helping them to be grateful for the little things each day, taking the positive aspects from the day and, above all, growing their patience and toleration of life's frustrations.

Part IV

Strengthen the intellectual brain

19

Intellectual development

Learning is the only thing the mind never exhausts, never fears, and never regrets.

(Leonardo da Vinci)

Intellectual abilities are almost exclusively controlled by the cerebral cortex, which is the outermost region of the brain, and which is identified by its folds and endless wrinkles. As we have already seen, the intellectual brain has less prominence in the child than in the adult. A baby is born with barely any wrinkles and they relate to the world primarily from the emotional brain. As the child learns and develops new skills, hundreds of billions of synapses, or nerve connections, begin to appear. These give the adult brain its volume and characteristic wrinkles. Each time the child learns something – such as discovering that when they let go of their dummy it will fall to the ground and make a noise – their brain develops new connections.

The world around them is the best teacher for the intellectual brain, and in this sense the most important thing for the child is to have opportunities to explore in different environments and with different people. We as parents make a modest contribution to their intellectual development, although a highly important one, since we are the ones who are principally responsible for the acquisition of language, as well as understanding the norms, customs and useful knowledge about our cultures. Any Inuit parent will teach their child their language, how to handle sled dogs, as well as the difference between a harpoon for seals and one for whales. What you teach your child may not have much in common with those of an Inuit parent, for example, but you will both try to successfully share the important points to allow your child to live in their culture.

As well as this transfer of customs and knowledge, parents also have a key influence on the intellectual development of their children, because as we know, we transmit a style of thinking. The style in which the child organises memories, makes up stories, or thinks about the future is transmitted

DOI: 10.4324/9781003360117-24

from their parents; therefore, the parents are contributing in an invaluable way to the child's intellectual development. From my experience, it is not surprising that the key to the brain potential of the child is in the relationship between parents and children. For the human brain there is no more complex stimulus than another human being. Interpreting the inflections of the voice, facial micro-expressions, the grammar used in their sentences or the motivations of other human beings are unique challenges. Despite this, many parents are fooled by stimulation programmes found on tablets or smartphones, thinking that they can be a beneficial stimulus for the child, more than a long conversation between parent and child. These parents are perhaps unaware that the human brain is much more complex, versatile, and effective than any computer that has been invented to date. The following comparison perfectly illustrates the inimitable richness of the human brain compared to a home computer, which tries to play a part in the education of children: the number of operations that a tablet, the type used by millions of children around the world – an iPad 2, for example – is 170 megaflops (a measure of the speed of a computer). In the same period of time, the human brain performs 2,200 million megaflops. In other words, the human brain is twelve million times more complex than an iPad 2. If computers had a beneficial effect on intelligence, you would have noticed that since the year 2000 – the year after which internet use began to grow – and more so since 2010 – when the popularity of smart phones exploded – you would have become a little smarter every year. Although this would be wonderful, I'm positive you don't have this feeling. However, if you are indeed a frequent user of this technology, it is likely that you are now less patient when you have to wait for something, you get bored more easily, and you find it hard to sit for a while in the park without looking at your mobile phone. As you can see for yourself, technology has not had a positive effect on your brain, it has actually made you less patient. Perhaps you also suffer from neck pain and have lost visual acuity. If you would like to share these "benefits" with your children's developing brain, you just have to download all the applications designed to grab children's attention and leave the electronic devices within reach. Personally, I am convinced that within a few years, all this technology will be sold with a large leaflet specifying the health risks and side effects.

Beyond the fact that technology does not appear to have any beneficial effect on the child's brain, I feel it is convenient to explain in this introduction what we understand today as intellectual capacity. Many people identify intellectual capacity by means of their intelligence quotient (IQ). The IQ is an invention of the early 20th century, designed to classify children according to their level of intelligence and give specialist attention to those who needed it. The first criticism of this system was that children with greater levels of difficulties were segregated from the normal education system in order to receive a special education. Nowadays, IQs receive considerable criticism because they do not assess all intellectual abilities, and what they do measure does not correspond to the conception we have of "intelligence" in the present day. Traditionally, someone who is highly educated, with deep cultural knowledge was identified as intelligent, but today most experts would give this role to a less cultured, more astute person. The reason is very simple, a person can accumulate a lot of knowledge and be very intelligent yet may find it hard to adapt to new situations or to achieve their goals. They will therefore be overtaken by other people who are brighter, or who have the gift of good timing. As you can see, intelligence has many nuances. Possibly the best definition we have of it is "the ability to solve new problems and adapt to the environment." Although this best defines the concept of intelligence, the intelligence quotient is actually the measurement that most relates to a person's level of development academically, socio-economicall, y and with regard to work. What I mean by this, is that it is very important to be smart, astute, or "on the ball", as we say in colloquial terms, but studies show that nurturing the mind and having a broad cultural knowledge is just as crucial. In this case, and as in many other areas of development, a good balance is best. Having a good balance between knowledge and intelligence offers greater advantages. I think it is just as important to help the child develop their more mischievous side, as it is to nurture their knowledge in all disciplines of life.

An ability to solve problems is not the only tool available to the intellectual brain. I use the word "tool" because from the point of view of the brain, all these abilities are nothing more than tools that allow us to survive and help us to achieve full development. The ability to deal with situations and concentrate, master language, memory, visual or executive intelligence are intellectual skills that we often overlook, yet they decisively influence our way of thinking, solving problems, making decisions or achieving those goals that we strive for in life. A child with developed visual intelligence will be able to solve problems more intuitively. The child with memory will be able to recall similar situations that allow him or her to solve a problem quickly. The attentive child will be able to pay attention to those details that make a difference and will remain focused until the end. The child who has a good grasp of language will be able to present their arguments and opinions in a clear and convincing way, and the child who has self-control will be able to wait for the ideal moment to take advantage of opportunities. The child who nurtures all these skills and who knows how to apply them will undoubtedly have many advantages in life. In this last part of the book we are going to review the most important tools of the intellectual brain, as well as providing practical and simple strategies to support your children in their development. At this point, you can assume that you will not find complex riddles or exercise charts. It is proven that computer programmes designed to train children's intellect have no (positive) effect on their intelligence, since they do not reproduce the way in which the child learns and develops.

Here you will find practical ideas so that in your routines and conversations you can have fun with your child and play at thinking, remembering or dealing with situations, so that they can boost the natural way in which their brain is developing. We are going to focus on six areas that experts agree are the most important in the child's intellectual development.

20

Attention

Success in life does not depend as much on talent, as on the ability to concentrate and persevere in what you want.

(Charles W. Wendte)

Attention is the window through which we communicate with the world. I want you to imagine that you are going to visit three houses with the intention of choosing one to buy. The first house has a spacious living room, with a single window. The window is so small that you have to move around to see the whole landscape and it reduces the brightness of the room. In the second house, there is a large stained-glass window in the living room. At first you find it very attractive and captivating, but the numerous pieces of glass and colours prevent you having a clear view of the outside, it fragments your attention and makes the room quite dark. In the third room, you find a large window that offers incredible views of the outdoors, allowing an abundance of light to come inside. Immediately you feel like sitting down to look at the landscape, or reading a book and sitting comfortably beneath the window. Attention is exactly the same as these windows placed in a room. When our attention is narrow, it is hard to have a good view of things and it is also hard to collect information coming in from outside. When our attention is fragmented, it is hard for us to concentrate and make good use of the outside light. However, when our attention is undivided and calm, we concentrate better, we are able to perceive all the details of the world around us and we can clearly learn the knowledge of the outside world.

Wide attention

Adults take courses in relaxation, yoga, or Tai Chi to maintain a wide attention, in an effort to have a brilliant and astute mind. Others practise mindfulness, a practice that we know improves their concentration, creativity, decision making and productivity. However, parents around the world continue to download games and apps on their mobile phones, in the hope of

DOI: 10.4324/9781003360117-25

making the attention span of their children ever faster. Why would anyone want to train their children to have a smaller, shorter or fragmented window to the outside world? In all honesty, I don't know. It surely has something to do with the widespread idea that video games and apps for children exercise the mind and enhance brain development. However, we now know that mobile apps, video games and television have no positive effect on the brain. Perhaps there will be some poorly informed reader, or a friend to whom you tell what you just read, who will tell you that it has been proven that apps for children improve the speed of decision making or visuospatial ability. Indeed, there are some studies that do indicate this. As an expert, I can assure you that the ones that I have come across are poorly designed, misdirected, and misinterpreted. The only thing these studies show is that the children who practise these games become faster and better at them. There are, however, many other studies that indicate that children who are in regular contact with mobile phone screens, tablets or computers are more irritable and have worse attention, memory and concentration than those who do not use them.

Slow attention

Another reason why many parents leave their children to play with video games is because, somehow, they need their children to grow up more quickly. When the child should be learning to draw straight lines with a pencil, the parents want them to be able to use a tablet, and when they should be playing freely and creating worlds of wizards and princesses, they want them to be the best at driving a motorbike in a videogame. Many are convinced that video games make children faster, as if this were a better way to grow up. If you intend to increase the speed of their attention, it's important to know that it is an intellectual capacity that must be developed gradually. A child begins by paying attention to an object for short periods of time and whenever that stimulus moves or makes sounds. Later on, the child is able to focus their attention for a longer period of time and more voluntarily; they no longer need the stimulus to move, emit lights or sounds. Beyond this, the child will learn to control their attention voluntarily; they will be able to remain quieter and start playing on their own for longer periods. At that time, many parents begin to encourage the use of mobile phones and tablets, with games in which the child has to blow up flying pigs, move motorbikes from here to there, or find angry birds that move across the screen. Rather than moving towards a greater attention span and greater control of the child's own mind, in my opinion it provokes a delay, as we are returning to the model in which the child does nothing but respond to sounds, movements and light signals. The only difference is that the speed at which objects move, and at which they change, is much faster. It would be like giving an 800 cc motorbike to a child who has just learnt to walk.

The value of attention

There is another, perhaps more powerful, reason why I don't think letting such young children entertain themselves with this type of technology is positive for their brains. There is a region in the emotional brain called the "corpus striatum" that has great relevance in terms of the development of our tastes and desires. This area, closely linked to attention, identifies which activities or games are better according to two principal factors. The first is the intensity of the stimulus, and the second is the speed at which the satisfaction comes. The more original, rewarding, remarkable or quick the stimulus is, the more "in love" the striated core of that activity will be. The problem is that the striated nucleus can only be filled with a few objects of desire, such as the person who is madly in love and can only think about the person they are in love with. Therefore the child who is captivated by the exciting world of tablets and video games may lose all interest in other things, such as having a conversation with their parents, playing with dolls or riding their bike, not to mention paying attention to their teacher or doing their homework. These children may seem inattentive and may be diagnosed with attention deficit disorder (ADD), when in reality what they have is little or no motivation. In the same way that children who are addicted to sweets lose their taste for other food which is less sweet – foods that in other eras and in other cultures were, and are, genuine treats, such as fruit – the child who plays video games runs the risk of losing their excitement for everything else. The problem can only get worse over the years; the only sufficiently rewarding stimuli that can make the striated nucleus forget about its love for screens and video games, are drugs, gambling and sex. It may seem harsh, but as I mentioned at the beginning of the book, the brain does not work as we believe or want it to work; it works as it works. The striated nucleus

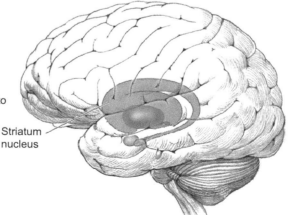

Striatum nucleus
- Concentration
- Assigning emotional value to things
- Taking decisions

Striatum
nucleus

is a structure that must be well monitored and protected, because it plays a very important role in addictive disorders and attention deficit. Just as a cook must educate their palate, parents must include educating their children's emotional palate on their list of duties. They must taste and enjoy all the nuances and textures of life before being exposed to stimuli that are so powerful that even adults feel helpless before them.

The truth is that I am not the only one who thinks this way about electronic devices. I could cite other colleagues or education experts who advocate limiting exposure time to these devices. However, it is easy for you to picture us all as eccentric researchers against technology. So, I prefer to provide you with some more telling examples. I hope their experiences seem relevant enough. In 2010, when a journalist asked Steve Jobs what his daughters' – aged fifteen and twelve – favourite iPad apps were, he replied: "They haven't used one yet. My wife and I limit how much technology our children use". Bill Gates is also very restrictive regarding his children's use of screens. Gates did not allow his children to use the computer or the internet until they were ten years old. Once they could access screens, they did so under strict conditions. Forty-five minutes from Monday to Friday, and one hour per day at the weekend. I don't think it's possible to give a more relevant example than that of Steve Jobs and Bill Gates. This trend is actually very common among executives from large technology corporations. In October 2011, *The New York Times* published an article entitled "A Silicon Valley School That Doesn't Compute". At the Waldorf Peninsula school, located in the centre of the Silicon Valley, students learn the old-fashioned way. They do not have electronic whiteboards or use keyboards to take notes. Instead, students get their hands covered in chalk and cross out all the mistakes they make in their notebooks with a pen. They spend time gardening, painting, and also reflecting. The most curious thing about this school is that the students who fill the classrooms are the children of the executives of the large Valley companies, including Apple, Yahoo, Google, and Facebook. These parents prefer their children to learn the traditional way, because they know that new technologies do not favour brain development of children.

Evidence on the effects of exposing young children to these types of stimuli – television, video games, smartphones, tablets – is significant. The American Academy of Pediatrics recommends that children under six years of age do not use screens, and the Mayo Clinic – one of the most prestigious medical institutions in the United States – recommends limiting their use at these ages to prevent cases of attention deficit disorder. I may be wrong, but knowing what I know about neuroscience and intellectual development, I don't have any apps for children on my mobile phone or my tablet. Occasionally my children use the mobile phone to look through photos of our holiday, or the day we made a cake, and we do it together. Sometimes we look at a song with them and learn the dance moves, but they don't play games. We also limit their time in front of the television. I prefer to find a balance using my own intuition, which coincidentally is what the American Academy of Pediatrics and the Mayo Clinic both indicate.

The executives from the big technology companies have it clear, the American Academy of Pediatrics and the Mayo Clinic do as well. Are you also sure about it? In case you had any doubts, and since some parents will not cease in their efforts to use screens to carry out brain training with their children, I have decided to dedicate an entire chapter to the educational programmes and apps that I consider to be most appropriate for children aged between zero and six years. In it, I describe their main advantages and explain the qualities of each of them. You can use them with your children whenever you want, because they are 100 per cent safe.

Now that you know the kind of activities that can interfere with the full development of your child's attention, I am going to give you some simple strategies to support their development.

Spend time with your children

This is a simple strategy. Children who spend more time with hired caregivers also spend more time in front of the television. This is perhaps why attention deficit difficulties are widespread among upper-class families, in which the two parents spend long hours away from home and leave the children under the care of a caregiver. For many parents, however, it may be impossible to be at home for longer periods of time and they genuinely need someone there to help. For those parents I will share a trick that I use when, for two weeks during the summer, the children have a hired caregiver because they have started their school holidays and we are still working. Every morning before leaving for work, I unplug the television. I have found that when children spend the morning at home without television, they smile much more and fill their morning with various activities. Reducing television time and spending time with your child, playing with them, helping them to concentrate, is the best way to ensure your children's attention.

Allow them to let off steam

Dealing with and concentrating on things requires self-control. When the child has spent the whole day at school, respecting classroom rules and being with their classmates, the region of the brain that exercises self-control may be somewhat tired. To regain their ability to use it, this area needs a break. The best way to do this is to let the child play freely and to let off steam. It is shown that children who play freely in a park or who do sport, are able to channel their energy more effectively, significantly reducing the risk of ADD. Offer them a little time to let off steam and to play freely each day.

Avoid interruptions

Good attention means better concentration. If you want to prevent your child from becoming distracted by the smallest things, I recommend that you avoid being the person who disrupts their concentration. Perhaps the best advice I can give you is to respect the moments when your child is calm, looking at a story or is absorbed in their toys. These are moments of mindfulness and it is worth respecting them. You can also help them by respecting their space when playing with other children. If you feel an uncontrollable need to participate, do so, but try to follow the rules of the game instead of being the one deciding them. Finally, avoid interruptions when you are playing or chatting together; focus on one single activity, do not jump from one topic to another in the middle of the conversation or constantly change your activity when you play with the child. Respect the child's train of thought.

Help them to keep their attention calmly

The environment influences the degree of relaxation or excitation of the brain. You probably feel much calmer when you take a walk in the country-side than when you are in the middle of a big city. You can help your child develop calm attention by creating spaces and moments in which he or she can feel relaxed. If you are going to talk to the child, or if you are going to draw, do so during calm moments: when their little brother is asleep, before you start to cook, or when they have finished their afternoon snack. If you are going to do something that requires attention, such as reading a story or making a cake, avoid distractions. Try tidying up the table where you are going to work, remove unnecessary objects, remove toys from sight, or simply turn off the television. You can also play some soft relaxing music. Children love classical music or jazz, and it can help them focus as long as it has a soft rhythm. You can also practise some mindfulness exercises for children. Mindfulness is the ability to give your full attention to a particu-lar moment in time. You can lie on the grass and simply watch the clouds float by or see how the leaves move on the trees. You can sit in a park, close your eyes and try to listen to the different sounds around you. You can also lie the child on your chest so that they can listen to your heart or your breathing. When one of my children has trouble sleeping, we practise a very simple exercise, but it really helps them to relax. I simply ask them to try to catch the air. As it cannot be done with their hands, I ask them to catch it with their nose, the only condition being that they catch it very slowly, filling their tummy and then releasing it slowly. Any activity in which the child concentrates on what is happening at the same time, can help them to have a calmer attention, and will help them learn to concentrate and relax when they are older.

Help them to concentrate until the end

Concentration is the ability to keep your attention for the exact time it takes to finish what you are doing. Children tend to lose interest quickly and have trouble finishing things. You can help your child by avoiding them becoming distracted. When you see that they begin to lose the thread of what they are doing or are losing interest – perhaps they have already lost it – quickly redirect their attention to what they were doing. The idea is that, regardless of whether you are making a cake or a plasticine figure, try to get them to finish what you started together. Sometimes it is not possible because the child is tired, or the activity is too long for a child of their age to finish. When they start to get distracted, sit next to the child and help them to stay focused. When you see that they are already very tired, reach an agreement as to what the child must complete before finishing. When he or she reaches the point that you have agreed on, congratulate them. It is important that they feel satisfied with all the effort they have made.

Remember

Full attention is that which is undivided, calm and maintained until the end. Avoiding your child being in contact with screens is the first strategy in protecting the normal development of their attention. Helping them to stay focused, develop a conversation style without breaks in it, doing exercise or creating the relevant atmosphere can help them achieve it.

21

Memory

> If history were taught in the form of stories, it would never be forgotten.
> (Rudyard Kipling)

Having a good memory means being able to learn and remember things with ease. A child with a good memory learns faster, remembers more details and usually enjoys the learning process. Studying and learning are easy and stimulating tasks for them. I am sure that there is not one of you who would not like your children or students to improve their ability to learn and remember. However, from my experience, parents know very little about how to help their children develop their memory capacity. In most cases, they have not considered it, do not know how to do it, or trust in their child learning at school. Unfortunately, none of these approaches is very successful. We know that a child's memory is structured primarily during the first years of their life, and that parents have a leading role in structuring it. In this sense, I can assure you that your role as a parent in the development of your child's memory is crucial.

Helping your child to have a good memory will not only allow them to learn and remember better or be a better student in the future. Napoleon Bonaparte said that a mind without a memory is like an army without a garrison, and in many ways he was right. We know that memory is a very important function when solving problems; you are probably reading this book because in a new or moderately difficult situation such as raising your children, you recall other occasions when a good book or the advice of an expert has helped you. I also hope that in the near future, maybe tomorrow, you will remember some of the advice you have read in this book and use it to make a good decision related to the education of your children. In either case, your memory will have helped you to solve the problem more effectively. Memory is also key to helping your children fulfil their dreams and be happier because, as you will see below, this helps the child to have more self-confidence.

As with other cognitive skills, memory is influenced by our genes, but it can be taught and empowered thanks to the plasticity of the brain. When I

DOI: 10.4324/9781003360117-26

was ten years old, they performed an intelligence test at my school with all the children in my year – more than 120 – and I received the lowest score in the part of the test that dealt with the memory. Today I make a living helping people recover their memories, and I can proudly say that within a couple of minutes I will have learnt the names of twenty new students attending my courses. I can assure you that memory can be strengthened if the right strategies are used. In this chapter we will discover how the child's memory develops and how we can empower them to learn and remember more effectively, as well as how to develop a positive thinking style.

Narrate your child's life to them

We know that much of the child's memory development is to do with conversations between mother and child. When mothers talk to their children, they usually talk about the things that are happening, that have just happened, that have happened throughout the day and that happened days before. To do this, mothers make up little stories that serve both to capture the child's attention and to organise the events in an orderly manner. We call these stories "narratives". Let's see how they work.

Celia and her mummy meet a lady in the street who offers the girl a sweet. When they get home, the mum tells the girl's grandfather that she is very lucky because a very nice lady has given her a strawberry flavoured sweet. Two months later, they meet the same lady in the supermarket and the mother asks her daughter: "Do you remember this lady?". Celia replies: "Yes, she gave me a strawberry sweet". Story telling seems to be an intrinsic feature of our species. In all cultures parents tell stories to their children, and every culture has its own stories and legends that are passed down from generation to generation. For years, researchers have been interested in the reasons why human beings like to create stories so much. Most scientists bet on the fact that it's an effective way to remember the past and imagine the future. And what everyone agrees on is that speaking about one's own life and telling imaginary stories helps to structure and organise a child's memory.

The child will even make up their own stories to be able to remember them. From before the age of two, a child will tell short stories about what has caught their attention so they can remember it better. If the child has gone to the zoo, just after arriving home or before going to bed, they will tell their mother that "the bear waved his hand". This little story that the child made up will help them remember the bear and his wave more effectively. All mums and dads can strengthen that natural tendency to make up stories by creating narratives with their children about what they have experienced together: a birthday party, a visit to their grandparents or a walk to the supermarket. Your child will learn to remember in a clearer and more organised way.

Develop a positive–elaborative conversation style

We know that different parents have different ways of making up stories. Some stories are greatly elaborated, others are very descriptive, and there are stories that are more concise. Elaine Reese, from the University of Otago, in New Zealand, is the director of a group of researchers who have been studying mother–child conversation styles for more than twenty years. Their studies have found that a specific type of conversation during childhood favours memory and learning capacity in adolescence and adult life. This communicative style is characterised by great elaboration of the narratives, ordering the events by time, emphasising the details that happened and focusing the child's attention on those moments that were fun or positive. This style of conversation is called "positive–elaborative". Although these scientists have found that conversational styles are different between parents, and that these differences are innate, it has been shown that any parent can develop a positive–elaborative style with a little practice, and the adoption of this style of conversation has an impact on the development of the child's memory. These are the key elements to a positive– elaborative conversational style.

Memory organization

One of the secrets of excellent memory is order. I want you to imagine two drawers. One could be yours and the other your partner's. In one of the drawers, all the socks, underwear and accessories – such as belts, bracelets and watches – are scrupulously ordered. In the other, the unpaired socks are mixed up with the unfolded underwear and accessories; it's a complete mess. If you and your partner had to compete to see who will be the first to find a specific pair of socks, who do you think would find it first? I am sure we all agree that the tidy drawer makes us agile when it comes to finding things. The same thing happens with our memory. The more ordered the memories, the easier it is to find them. The child, however, does not have an orderly memory, and although they are able to remember many things, their memories appear in a separated manner. A three-year-old, for example, may remember several things that have happened over a weekend, but it will take a lot of work to differentiate between what happened on the first day and what happened on the second. In the child's mind, many events are uneven and stored without a logical or time order that makes it easier to recall the memory. Therefore, when we talk with a child about the past, it should be done in an orderly manner, as a sequence of stories that allows each event to be joined to the next. In this way the child will begin to remember in order, and that will allow them to access memories more easily. This simple technique will allow your child to develop a more agile, efficient memory.

Let's look at a narrative that William's mother makes for him when she realises that he can't remember the order of activities they had done together that afternoon. The boy is convinced that they bought the medicine after leaving the doctor and does not remember everything that happened. If memories are given a timeline, the child is not only able to remember the correct order of events, but is also able to recall parts of the afternoon that he did not remember.

First, we went to the doctor and he looked at your throat.

Afterwards, we went to the supermarket and we bought milk for breakfast.

And the last thing we did was to go to the chemist to buy the medicine.

Definition

When we create stories about the day, our holidays or the birthday party we have just been to, it is important to pay attention to the details. The child's memory fixates on general ideas, impressions, but few details. Their memory is like a big fishing net. You can catch large fish, but medium and small-sized fish will escape through the holes. Helping a child to remember small details will help them to develop an increasingly clear and defined memory. Something similar to what some call a "photographic memory". Giving clarity to a story is as simple as helping the child remember details that aren't necessarily relevant. For example, if your son remembers the chocolate cake and the crisps from his friend's party, you can say: "Yes, you loved the cake and the crisps, and you also ate a lot of breadsticks and olives, do you remember?" Or, for example, if your daughter tells you that she was playing with dolls at her friend's house, you can help her to remember the details: "Sophie, these pyjamas are the same colour as Alexandra's favourite doll's dress, aren't they? Do you remember what little things her doll wore? A tiara and a necklace? Very good!". You can add clarity to any memory if you review the details related to colours, shapes, objects, things your child did or those that others did.

Reach

Another interesting strategy is to help the child reach memories that are stored in remote places of their memory. We know that many of the things we have lived and experienced – and that we are not able to remember – are stored in our memory, but the brain is not able to access them by itself. Talking about the past and being able to thread together what has recently happened with more distant events, and in turn with the distant past, can help the memory develop a greater reach and agility in the recovery of memories. Let's look at a simple example of a conversation between Helen and her mother about delicious ice cream.

M: The ice cream we had today was delicious, wasn't it? H: Yes, mine was chocolate. M: Yes, and mine was strawberry.	M: Hey, and last week when we went to the park with your friends, Mary's mum also bought you an ice cream. Can you remember what flavour it was? H: Yes! It was mint.	M: And do you remember last summer we had lots of ice cream? H: No... M: We bought them by the beach, from a really nice man. H: Oh yes! And daddy's fell on the ground and a dog ate it!

A great way to help your children have a far-reaching memory is to talk to them every night about what happened during the day or to bring up different anecdotal circumstances that occurred in similar situations, as we have seen in the previous examples. In this way, the child will learn to recover their memories more easily.

Remember positively

Do you remember the first time you went on holiday with your friends? The first trip with your partner? Your child's first birthday? The memories you have of these moments probably have something in common: they are positive memories. The human brain has a natural tendency to remember positive moments and discard the bad ones. This helps us to be in a good mood, have a good concept of ourselves, and it also gives us self-confidence. You can take advantage of this when talking to your child about nice things from the past, such as the example of the ice cream. Any fact that is enjoyable, such as the taste of the ice cream – or a funny anecdote, such as dad's ice cream being devoured by a dog – will allow the child to access their memory more easily. Mums who communicate through an elaborative–positive style pay more attention to the fun or enjoyable details of memories, thus promoting the development of a better memory in the child.

Remembering the positives is also key to improving a child's confidence. The memories of our life, those experiences that for some reason deserve to be remembered, are stored in the "precuneus" region, an area of the posterior cerebral cortex. Each time the child – and then the adult – must make a decision as to whether to start a project or solve a problem, the brain searches in its precuneus memories to back the decision. If the precuneus contains positive memories and the child is able to access them, they will be more optimistic when taking on a challenge, facing it with more confidence. In a certain sense, the precuneus functions as a kind of curriculum vitae of our own life. When a CV shows experience in a given field, the candidate will present themselves for the job knowing they are the best candidate. In this sense, if Clare's mother helps her to remember that she defended herself from a friend who wanted to take away her doll, or was able to get dressed on her own, the next time that she is faced with a similar situation, the memories stored in her precuneus will help her to manage the task with complete confidence.

Precuneus

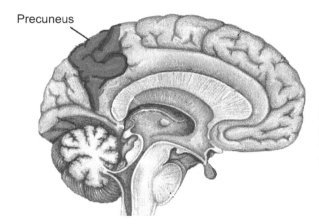

Precuneus
Memories of our life
• Memories of success
• Memories of failure

Remember the negative

Often, the child brings up unpleasant or unfair situations that happened during their day. It is important that you accommodate those memories. When the child talks about them it is because they hold real significance for the child and they want to understand them better. As we saw in the chapter about the importance of communicating the two hemispheres, it is important that you help your child integrate emotional experiences through talking about them. Another reason why it is necessary to acknowledge these memories for the child is because it may be important for their brain to remember them. Imagine that a boy hit your child at school or took a toy from them and did not want to give it back. More than it being just something that happens between children, your child wants to remember that it was this child in particular who hit them. I would want to remember who they were if it was me. Remembering mistakes and dangers is a sign of intelligence because it helps us to foresee and resolve problems in the future.

Remember

A child with a good memory is one who enjoys learning and remembering, who solves problems in a more effective way and who is able to make better decisions. You can help your child develop a more efficient memory if you talk to them about the past in an orderly way. You can also help them remember details that they cannot remember and recover anecdotes and experiences that are too far away for the child to bring them on their own. Do not forget to go over their most meaningful experiences at the end of the day and take advantage of their natural tendency to be more able to remember the positives, while paying attention to the negative memories that the child needs to talk about.

22

Language

> If you want your children to be intelligent, read them fairy tales. If you want them to be more intelligent, read them more fairy tales.
>
> (Attributed to Albert Einstein)

If there is a skill that the child's brain acquires in a similar way to how a sponge absorbs water, it is the ability to understand and express ideas and concepts through words. In an imperceptible way, the child spends their first months of life learning to discriminate between different sounds of the voice, seeking to understand where one word ends and the next begins and identifying those sounds with different objects, moments, situations and even feelings. Although their brain has spent almost a year associating sounds and ideas, in the eyes of the adult the child begins to understand as if by magic. From the magical moment in which the child is able to look at their mother when they hear the word "mummy", their brain begins to understand that, in some way, they are also capable of producing sounds, and in fact, every time they see you saying a word, their brain imagines how they should shape their mouth in order to reproduce the same sound. Gradually the child begins to control the position and the force with which they press their lips together to be able to say "daddy" or "mummy". From that moment on, the child's brain is busting with sounds, noises, words and meanings. By the time they are sixteen, the child will know more than 60,000 words, which means that they will have learned vocabulary at a rate of ten words per day. Though in actual fact, between the ages of two and five we know that the child acquires vocabulary at a rate of fifty words per day. It is difficult for us to understand how they can learn so many in such a short time, but the child's brain is incorporating every word they hear in every kind of conversation and context.

For thousands of years, different generations have transmitted their knowledge through language. However intelligent a doctor or an architect might be, they could not do their job if they had not received information from their ancestors about how to operate or build. Scientists agree that

DOI: 10.4324/9781003360117-27

language has been the key to allowing human beings to develop their full potential. In a similar way, language has an enormous significance in the development of your child's intelligence. Thanks to language, your child will be able to acquire knowledge and transmit it to others. It is the most important tool you will have throughout your life for learning, relating to others and getting what you want. When they write their letter to Father Christmas, take an exam or when the day comes when they declare their love to someone, language will be the tool that will allow them to achieve their dreams. That versatility of language, which helps us acquire knowledge and transmit ideas, is what makes it one of the most important skills for the development of intelligence. In fact, richness of vocabulary is the variable that most influences the intelligence quotient.

Although language is acquired, in a certain sense, and in a natural way, the truth is that from a cerebral point of view it is a tremendously complex task. At least six areas of the brain must be coordinated each time we say a word or interpret a text. These structures are located in the left hemisphere and perform tasks as diverse as analysing sounds, discriminating between them, interpreting their meaning, storing vocabulary, identifying written words, looking for words in the vocabulary storage, constructing sentences or making shapes with our lips, tongue and vocal cords that allow us to form words.

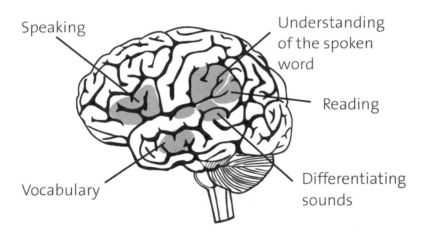

Speaking

Understanding of the spoken word

Reading

Vocabulary

Differentiating sounds

Left hemisphere

Essentially, while it is true that the child's brain absorbs vocabulary and the rules of language naturally, this would not happen without the help of adults. We know that parents have a great influence on the development of a function as complex as that of language. Their daily conversations contribute to enriching vocabulary, improving understanding and organising speech, but other aspects, such as their attitude towards reading, can make the child master language, a fundamental tool for navigating the world. I will now give you some strategies that can help your child develop a richer language.

Speak to them often

Speaking to a child is giving them the opportunity to learn the language. Experts agree that from the earliest moment in childhood, the more the child is exposed to new words, the greater their vocabulary. However, not all parents are equally talkative. Betty Hart and Todd Risley, of the University of Kansas, found that while some parents exchange roughly 300 words per hour with their child, others can reach 3,000. The data is very clear. In most cases, women speak much earlier and much more with their child than men do. This is due to a differentiation of roles seen from the very beginning of our times. While the men went out to hunt in small groups that advanced stealthily through the forest so as not to scare the animals, the women congregated in the village to take care of the children and talk animatedly. You only need to go to a park to see that times have not changed much. In all those that I go to, the same rule is visible. For every three or four mothers who are watching their children, there is usually only one father. This is not an observation; it is a fact. The greater specialisation of women in tasks of communication has equipped their brain, with some 200 million more neurons in the brain areas of the tongue than men, throughout evolution. This is perhaps the biggest difference between the brain of a man and that of a woman, and if you are a man, I urge you to observe how the women in your family communicate with the children.

From birth you can talk to your child, calmly, but in a fluid way. We fathers do not usually know what to say to an unresponsive baby, yet there are many things you can. You can describe what you are seeing in the room, explain what you are cooking, what you have done at work or simply explain what is going on in the football game. You can also stop for a minute to tell your child how you feel on that particular day. Remember that enriching the child's vocabulary of feelings will help them to develop their emotional intelligence. Try to talk to the child while facing them, so that they can look at you while you speak, as a great amount of speech development occurs through imitating the positions of the lips and tongue. The next time you talk to a child who is under one year of age, look at their eyes; they mainly concentrate on your mouth, in an instinctive attempt to learn how you make these fun noises that attract other people's attention.

Widen their universe

It is important not to limit communication to your close surroundings. Many parents spend the first months in a bubble, where the child's universe is limited to the house and the supermarket. But the child will enjoy being in different environments and with people who can enrich their linguistic abilities. Being exposed to objects and situations other than those found in the security of your own home will expand their vocabulary. It doesn't matter if you go to the ironmongers, to buy a carpet or to take care of a financial matter in the bank, take your baby with you and let them learn in the real world. Likewise, deciphering the sounds of different people, each with their own accent and pronunciation, will allow the child to refine their ability to incorporate the sounds of their language, and even other languages. Widening the social circle of your child will not only improve their capacity to understand messages, it will also enrich their vocabulary. To give you the simplest example, you may have a ceramic hob in your own home, and at your parents' house they have a gas cooker. This small difference will allow your child to be exposed to words such as "gas", "match" or "hob" when visiting your parents' house. Furthermore, if they live in another neighbourhood that you drive to, your child will hear the words "parking space", "parking metre" or "ticket". Contact with other people is a safe source of enriching their language, as each person with whom you come into contact will bring other worlds into your child's universe of language.

Another way to expand your universe is through songs and reading, as they are an effective way to expose the child to new words heard over and over again from early childhood. Bring back songs from your childhood and sing them with your child, get children's music playlists and listen to them at home or in the car. Children will learn the words by heart, and it will expand their vocabulary in an enjoyable way.

Play with instructions

This is a game that I occasionally play with my children and that all three enjoy. Each playing according to their age and complexity. Following instructions is somewhat more difficult than it may seem at first glance. To follow an instruction, the brain needs to put into motion a complex mechanism that is essentially the same as you have to follow when building a piece of Ikea furniture. First, you have to understand different parts of the message. To do this you have to recover different meanings from your memory. If, for example, the instructions say that you must insert the four *skungen* screws onto the back of the top shelf of a bookshelf, your brain will have to perform a complex process. First it must identify the *skungen* screws and differentiate them from the *fixa* or the *kløve* screws. Second, you must count up to four, separate them from the rest and avoid forgetting where you have put them. Then you must remember that you need to locate the top shelf and identify the back of it, according to the indications in the drawing. Only then can you retrieve the *skungen* screws and screw them into the piece of wood. For a one-year-old child, understanding that they must put their nappy in the bin can be just as complex. For a five-year-old, understanding that in order to make a pizza they must first add the tomato sauce, then the cheese, then finally the ingredients cut into small pieces, can be just as complicated as it is for you to build an Ikea bookcase.

This is why giving instructions can be a complex and stimulating game to improve your child's understanding and ability to work with words. You will be surprised at how difficult it can be to follow instructions when you set the table with them, get the child's schoolbag ready with them, or simply when you are helping them to put away their toys.

A sentence as simple as "Put your cars away in the big box" will require a huge effort from a two-year-old child, and a somewhat more complex sentence such as "Pour the milk into the cup, put two spoons on the table and look for two napkins in the second drawer", is going to be a challenge for a child of five. In addition to practising with everyday tasks, you can also play with your children by giving them fun instructions such as "Jump in the air, clap, then do a somersault. Ready?". Both for games and everyday life, adjust the length and complexity of the instructions according to the capabilities of your own child, and repeat them as many times as necessary so that the child understands what they should do. If you help them pay full attention when you are giving them instructions and also when you notice that they have not understood or retained the entire message, you will see how quickly they progress. Helping your child to follow instructions will allow them to improve their ability to concentrate and to work mentally with language. It is also a fantastic way to develop responsibility and collaboration in household tasks.

Expand their sentences

Language is not just vocabulary. Grammar allows us to combine words and construct meanings, and is a somewhat more difficult function to acquire. One of the most interesting aspects of grammar is that if the same words are combined in different ways, we can create totally different meanings. For example, the phrase "Valerie doesn't want crisps because she is annoyed", has a different meaning than "Valerie is annoyed because she doesn't want crisps". In the first case, sadness is a cause and in the second it is a consequence. In the case of her not wanting crisps because she is annoyed, her older sister will try to comfort Valerie by giving her a hug. On the other hand, if Valerie is angry because she does not want crisps, her sister may offer to exchange them for her breadsticks, because she has understood perfectly that crisps were the problem.

Reaching a conclusion like that of Valerie's older sister, requires mastering the rules of language, though it is something a child of about four or five years old can attain. However, there is a big difference between being able to understand the rules of language and being able to use them to construct sentences and paragraphs that convey exactly what the child means. When the child reaches two years of age, we can help them broaden their expressions by adding adjectives or verbs. For example, if our son points to a dog that runs behind some pigeons and says: "A dog", we can give a slightly wider reply which includes a verb, an adjective and an adverb: "Yes! It is a very playful dog". As the child grows, we can expand their sentences in a more extensive way if we help them to add content or make more complex phrases, such as those in the following examples:

GABRIELLE: I saw a squirrel.

MUM: Yes!! We saw a red squirrel climbing up the tree to collect pinecones, didn't we?

MARTIN: Daddy's car has "broke" down.

DADDY: Yes, you're right, daddy's car has broken down and we have taken it to the mechanic.

As you can see, the father does not point out the child's mistakes, he simply returns the same message in the correct way. Language acquisition experts claim that unless it is a very repetitive mistake, correcting the child's sentences without explicitly pointing out that he or she has made a mistake is the best way to help them internalise grammar and to use it properly. It will also avoid them feeling insecure in their use of language.

Instil a love of reading in your children

There is a proverb that says, if you are able to read this phrase, you should thank a teacher. Yes, you do learn to read at school, but a love for reading is, without doubt, a seed that is sown and nurtured by parents. There are many courses that promise to teach reading at three or four years of age. There is no study to indicate that learning to read at such early ages benefits the child in any way. However, we do know that children who enjoy reading, and those who grow up loving books, have a richer vocabulary, are more able to understand what they read, write better, and have fewer spelling mistakes. My editor likes to mention another piece of information that will certainly interest you. According to the latest data collected in the PISA report – an international analysis of student performance – children who live in houses where there are 200 books or more, obtain a 25 per cent higher performance at school than those living in houses with ten books or less. It is not surprising that in 2015, the winner of the Global Teacher Prize (equivalent to the Nobel Prize for teachers and professors) was awarded to Nancie Atwell, a teacher whose main virtue has been to instil a love for reading in her students, getting them to read an average of forty books a year, compared to the average of eight that they read in other schools. This means that her students read a different book each week. A few days before the award was given to her, this teacher from Maine in the United States revealed the secret of her success in an interview: "It is nothing more than allowing the child to choose the book that they most want to read". Simple, isn't it?

Reading time is a magical moment for the parent and their child. Children whose parents read stories with them every day know more words, have the agility to recognise written words and acquire the habit of reading every day. Try to make this a special moment; let your children choose the story they want you to read them, be enthusiastic and act out the characters. I know that tiredness can make this time require additional effort and that, on many occasions, sleep can take hold of you. However, it is worth the effort. In addition, the short time the story takes offers a unique opportunity to build a bond and their memory. When we are lying with our child or holding them in our arms, the contact of our bodies and the good night kiss will help generate oxytocin, which if you remember is the hormone of love, the one that makes us feel united with another person and safe. Reading a story is also my favourite time to immerse myself in the world of memories, and I try to help them develop a positive thinking style. Every night before bed, we look over the day, adding details to their memories and we try to find two or three good or enjoyable aspects of the day.

Remember

Language is a complex function and the main tool for your child to function successfully in school and in life. Speak to them, expand their vocabulary and phrases, correct them without pointing out their mistakes and dedicate a short time every day to reading. You will help them to master the tools of language and foster a love of reading that will grow stronger. You will give them a safe path to look out onto the world and develop their intelligence. I'd like to bring this chapter to a close by inviting you to look for classic stories, unique stories and fun stories, and to enjoy story time with your child this very evening.

23

Visual intelligence

> Studies have shown that 90% of error in thinking is due to error in perception.
>
> (Edward de Bono)

Spatial function is the ability to perceive and interpret the shapes and space around us. It is the ability you use when your child asks you to draw a dragon, for example. If you are now recalling your line drawing classes and you are thinking that this type of skill is what an architect or an engineer uses to make plans and design objects, you are right. Many parents pay little or no attention to this way of perceiving and thinking, since they consider it a component of intelligence that is not very useful for real life, unless working as precisely as an architect or an engineer. As you will now be able to understand, they could not be more wrong. The ability to perceive, interpret and construct figures in a space is one of the six key areas that can contribute to your child's intellectual development. Although it may seem that only designers and architects need this ability in their day-to-day lives, in reality, we all use our spatial skills more frequently, and in more areas, than we believe. Let's look at some examples. Of course, all tasks involving crafts or drawing are supported by your child's ability to imagine spatial relationships, but many other skills also depend on this ability. Surely you would like your child to have neat and tidy handwriting. It is also highly likely that you would prefer your child not to be overwhelmed by maths throughout their school career, don't you agree? It turns out that relatively simple tasks, such as knowing which direction the letters face when writing, how to arrange the numbers when solving a problem or doing a simple addition with carry overs can be an impossible mission if the child is not able to mentally master their space.

But, beyond specifically applying it to one area of study or another, thinking in the form of images makes it easier for the child to develop a different type of logical thinking, which we all know about. When we think with words, our mind follows a logical discourse, which is bound by the laws of

DOI: 10.4324/9781003360117-28

grammar. However, when we think of images, we do so in a more intuitive way. It is the kind of intelligence that allows us to suss someone out as soon as we meet them, to know how to solve a problem without understanding how we got there, and also – one for the dads – to know where best to place the ball to allow another player to score a goal. Another reason why spatial skills are so relevant in the child's intellectual development is that they are closely linked to social intelligence or, in other words, your child's ability to be successful in social relationships. Each time your child finds themselves in front of another person, his or her brain will unconsciously interpret each of their gestures, grimaces, expressions and silences to be able to interpret how far they trust what they are saying, or if they have ulterior motives. This is all because the brain does not see reality as it is; it must interpret it. If you see your husband in profile, you cannot see the side hiding behind his silhouette, but your brain interprets that the rest of him is there. In the same way, when we see a car, it is unlikely we will see all of it. We will probably see the front end of it, and one of the sides, but immediately the brain interprets that it is complete car. When interpreting faces, the brain has to make an extra effort. The brain can fix its attention on different features of the face, such as the shape of the mouth and eyes, and from this information it can interpret what emotions the person is experiencing, or the intentions they have. In this sense, the right part of the brain is responsible for bringing all the independent parts together to make sense of it all, like when your child builds a house with Lego®. In this way, the child can differentiate their father from their uncle, because one has a beard and the other does not, or tell when their mother is angry, joking or serious, because each emotion is associated with a different facial expression. In the following illustration, you can see the process of interpretation that the child's brain has to perform when interpreting the facial expression of another person.

Different studies with preschool children have shown that various techniques and strategies can help the child develop the ability to understand and master spatial relationships between objects, in order to interpret faces more effectively, or develop, among other things, neater, tidier handwriting. Here are my favourites.

Play at building

Construction games are the main tool for parents who want to help their children improve their ability to perceive and build figures in a space. Jigsaws, Lego® or the classic building block game will delight any child. However, there are many other enjoyable games and strategies that will help them to understand and reason with shapes and spaces.

Allow the child to become familiar with visual language

Taking into account the enormous plasticity of the brain in terms of language, you can help your child to better understand the space if you use words that refer to the way different objects occupy the space that surrounds them. You can use adjectives that describe their size (large, small, tall, short, fat, skinny, thick, thin, tiny), their shape (curved, straight, pointed, blunt, circular, rectangular, oval) or their state (full, empty, squint). You can also point out the relation of objects to their space using prepositions. So, instead of saying, "I'm going to put the toy here", you can try something a little more spatial like, "I'm going to put the toy on the table", or instead of saying, "The doll has been tidied away", you can say: "The doll has been tidied away in the cupboard next to the coats".

Difference between right and left

Our brain always takes our own body as a reference to guide itself. If I tell you to think of the "north" cardinal point, you will most likely think of looking in front of you, or even above your head. If you do know where north is, you may have turned to orientate yourself, so that the cardinal point is facing you. A first step to encourage orientation with respect to the body itself is to teach the child to be able to differentiate between right and left. Instead of turning the corner and saying, "Let's go this way", we can say, "We're going to go down the street on the right". We can also tell the child that the spoon is on their right, ask them to raise their left hand or help them to think which side the letter "b" faces.

Help them with spatial thinking

Helping your child to reason with space is great for them to be able to understand relationships between objects. You only need to get your child dressed and take them to buy the groceries to ask them things like: "Which way do you put on your trousers?", "Which is further away, the supermarket or your school?", "Do you think the watermelon will fit into this bag?", "Which takes up more space, this banana or these four apples?".

Play at making maps

Many people will think it's crazy to play and interpret maps with a child of three or four years old. However, they find it fascinating and fun. Obviously, you cannot start with a metro map of a large city; the most convenient and entertaining way for children is to start by drawing a plan of the room where you are. Start by drawing the floor – the shape of the room – and then draw the sofa or chair where you are sitting.

From there, the child can tell you where in the picture is the door and where is the window, the bookshelf or the television. In this simple way, children learn to interpret a floor plan perfectly. Another day you can do the same, but in a different room, such as the kitchen or their bedroom, and little by little you can keep going until you are drawing a plan of your entire home and the route you take to get to school. If you take public transport, looking at the route on a map can be a great way for the child to understand that the drawing is what they see every day with their own eyes. You can also play with a map of the world. You can talk about the different countries and the characters in them. Peter Pan in London, Ratatouille in Paris, Aladdin in Arabia and Pocahontas in the United States. There are countless characters, animals, trees or natural settings that your child will quickly relate to in every place in the world.

Apps and video games

You will have probably read in some newspaper article that video games are fantastic for developing the visual perceptual skills of the child. Apps provide all kinds of games and puzzles for your child to squeeze the most out of their neurons. The truth is that I cannot recall any scientific article which says that playing these apps leads to greater visual perceptual skills. There are three articles that relate to playing video games with a greater speed in detecting and processing visual information, but they are studies conducted with older children. There is no evidence in favour of their use in young children, yet there is evidence against it. However, video games are always a temptation for both children and parents. The challenge is to choose one that is suitable for a child under six years old. Remember that in Chapter 26 you have a complete list of all video games and apps for smartphones and tablets that can, in my opinion, be beneficial for a child between zero and six years of age. Don't hesitate to consult the list as many times as you need to.

Play at making faces

Children love to make faces, especially if it is an excuse to make funny faces and laugh. It has been proven that deciphering and interpreting emotional expressions helps in developing social intelligence. You can play at making faces while they have dinner or when they brush their teeth. When the child is only two years old, you can begin to have a happy, sad, angry or surprised face and, little by little, increase the repertoire with more complex emotions, such as indecision, boredom or nervousness. The two favourite faces of any child and which should not be missed out on at any age, are the monster and the crazy face!

Remember

Perception is the door through which we interpret the world. The benefits of being able to reason both visually and spatially will help your child to draw and write better, master mathematics, interpret other people's expressions and develop a more intuitive thinking style. Play with your child to understand and master spatial relationships; they will grasp it.

24

Self-control

He who controls others may be powerful, but he who has mastered himself is mightier still.

(Tao Te Ching – Lao Tse)

In the 1960s, Walter Mischel, a psychologist at Stanford University, devised a Machiavellian experiment to test the self-control of children between four and six years of age. The experiment was very simple: each child was seated on a chair in front of a table where there was a plate with a marshmallow. The researcher gave the child very simple instructions: "You can eat the marshmallow if you want, but if you wait fifteen minutes without eating it, I will give you another one. Then you can eat two marshmallows instead of one". As soon as the researcher left the room, it became clear that the task was more difficult for the children than one would initially think. Signs of agitation were immediately visible, with children scratching their heads, bouncing their legs up and down. There were those who swayed from left to right and those who did it forwards and backwards like a rocking chair. Some gave the marshmallow a furtive glance, and others stared at it. Almost all of them touched the sweet several times with their left hand – that which controls the most impulsive and emotional hemisphere – while covering their eyes with the right hand, which is controlled by the rational hemisphere. Approximately one-third of them overcame the challenge thanks to a titanic effort of self-control. The rest of the group, although they tried with all their might, could not resist the temptation in the fifteen minutes needed to get the second marshmallow. This experiment shows how tremendously difficult it is for the brain to exercise self-control. To achieve it, the frontal lobe must assume absolute control, dominate the emotional and instinctive part of the brain and fight frustration and hunger. In order to exercise this control, the frontal lobe needs to consume large amounts of glucose. The longer the frontal lobe makes the effort to avoid the sweet, the more sugar it demands, which makes the sweet more and more appetising, turning it into a gruelling struggle between the two forces. If you've ever gone on a diet

DOI: 10.4324/9781003360117-29

or quit smoking, you'll know what I'm talking about. The reality is, that whatever the task, exercising self-control is really difficult for the brain; a high-level skill that requires lifelong training.

The most interesting thing about this research, however, is what happened several years after the experiment. Investigators called the children's parents about fifteen years later – the children were then between nineteen and twenty-one – and collected diverse information about their academic and social lives. To the surprise of the researchers, the number of minutes the child had lasted without eating the marshmallow was closely related to their selectivity scores and their average school results. Children who displayed more self-control in preschool obtained better academic results throughout their entire school career. Upon reaching adulthood, the parents of these children described them as responsible and easy to deal with, much more than those who could not wait. Different studies have replicated this research, and they all reach the same conclusion: the greater the child's ability to control themselves, the greater their academic achievements and social integration.

Executive intelligence

Self-control is one of the intellectual capacities that falls within what we know as "executive intelligence". Executive intelligence is the set of skills that allow the person to decide on goals, make plans to achieve them, carry out these plans and evaluate the results. In a sense, executive intelligence carries out the functions of an orchestra conductor that directs the different instruments that are available to the brain, and takes control over which should be played at any given time. The frontal part of the brain, the one that internalises the rules, also exercises the capacity of self-control, which helps resolve problems according to the established rules and allows the rational brain to take control of the emotional brain when necessary. These functions, the most complex of those exercised by the human brain, are mainly formed during adolescence and adulthood, although from a very young age we begin to lay the foundations of their development by nurturing self-control, exercising responsibilities, learning from our own decisions and controlling our actions.

In this way, as with the experiment we have just seen, the child who develops their executive intelligence is able to control themselves and not spend the pocket money their mother has just given them in the first shop they come to; instead they are able to wait until they reach a different shop which sells the stickers they prefer. Again you can see here that the ability to tolerate frustration and connect the emotional brain with the rational one allows the child to meet their needs more successfully. A greater capacity for self-control is also fundamental to the prevention of behavioural disorders and the prevention and treatment of the dreaded attention deficit disorder.

In both cases, the root of the problem lies in having poor control capabilities, which does not allow the child to take control of their anger, frustration or concentration. But how can we help the child gain self-control? One option would be to buy a bag of marshmallows and practise fifteen minutes each day. This, I'm afraid, would result in too much sugar and would be ineffective. Here are several strategies that will help you cultivate self-control on a day-to-day basis.

Overcome frustration

One thing you can do with your child from a very young age is to help them control their frustration, little by little. To achieve this there is no choice but to expose your child to a certain level of frustration. Try to answer their needs promptly, but not urgently. Trust your baby. They can withstand a little discomfort. When they need their nappy changed, when they want to be fed or when they should be put to bed because they are tired, go to meet their needs, but avoid becoming agitated; you will only teach them that experiencing discomfort is distressing. When they are agitated, help to calm them down, so that they will learn to do it without your help some day. Take them in your arms so they feel protected. Be very calm and talk to them or sing softly to them. Tell them peacefully and confidently that they will get what they are waiting for; help them to concentrate on something else to distract them from the discomfort. Try to be by their side without feeling distress or guilt, but rather confidence and empathy.

As the child grows up, be sure to set limits that they must respect. Household rules, rules at the table and schedules for watching television will help their brain understand that they cannot always have everything. It will serve as training for learning how to calm down when they are frustrated. Remember that when it comes to setting limits it is very important that you yourself are calm and show warmth. It is also important that you understand that it is not good for you to impose more rules than the child's brain can manage. Offer them some time free from rules – or with fewer rules – as well as physical activities that help them channel all their energy and frustration into appropriate situations.

Help them be in control of the present

For a child, performing relatively simple tasks such as getting dressed or putting away their toys can be very complicated. Tasks such as this are composed of small steps that the child has to do in sequence, and this can be complicated for them. To help the child be in control of the present we can offer some support, such as giving them instructions, step by step, asking them to say out loud what they are going to do or making it easier by dividing a more complex task into smaller ones. If they can think in logical sequences, they may feel that they are in control of the situation, instead of being overwhelmed by it. Let's look at an example. Tomorrow is Andrew's mother's birthday and he is determined to make her a delicious cake. He knows that he has to make it with yoghurt, sugar and egg, and that he needs a large bowl to mix everything. However, he doesn't know where to start. Fortunately, his father is there to divide the task into smaller steps, thus turning a difficult task into something easy.

First, we are going to clean the table so that everything is tidy.	Then we are going to take out the ingredients and the mixing bowl.	Then we are going to wash our hands and we can start cooking.

With this simple explanation, Andrew knows where to start and can take control of his job as a dedicated cook. If we teach our children to perform tasks in an organised way, we prevent them from feeling lost, we help them gain self-control, and we also increase their abilities to solve complex problems. This is because we know that people who are more able to deal with complex tasks are characterised by effective organisation and their ability to divide difficult tasks into different steps. You can check the effectiveness of this strategy by inviting your child to solve a jigsaw puzzle in three simple steps.

First, we are going put all the pieces facing up.	Then we are going to look for the four corner pieces and put them in place.	We then add the pieces that go around the edge, and then we add the rest.

The strategy always works the same, regardless of whether we are going to make a cake, do a jigsaw puzzle or design birthday invitations. Clearing the area to work (prepare), deciding which part we want to start with (prioritise) and then deciding how we are going to continue (planning) will allow the child to acquire the control they need to realise their proposal, gaining results that fill the child with satisfaction.

Control the future

One of the most defining skills in human evolution has been our ability to know the future. Our ancestors learnt to read footprints so that they could picture the whereabouts of the animals they hunted. Nowadays, we anticipate the weather, changes in the political cycle or the evolution of diseases with the sole purpose of controlling our destiny. On a smaller scale, people who are able to anticipate difficulties, save, or work today to receive the rewards tomorrow, also experience such benefits, just as the children who received two marshmallows instead of one. Teaching them to think about the future can be part of the daily life of all children. In many situations, it is a simple case of putting into words what we are doing and talking to your child about tomorrow. For example, Julia's mother can say to her in the morning: "We are going to leave your dummy on your pillow for when we go to sleep", and at night "We are going to go to the toilet before going to sleep so we don't have an accident in the bed". Mark's dad can help his son get his own school bag ready, packing away his coloured pencils and the snack he will need during the day. We can also help the child to anticipate the consequences of their actions, making them see what can happen if they act in one way or another.

Losing control

An important and beautiful part of self-control is knowing when it is good to exercise it and when it is not. You will agree with me that self-control can be a real obstacle during a night of passion with your partner, or when celebrating a pay rise. The frontal lobe is the organ responsible for exercising not only self-control but deciding when it should be applied. It would be of little use to teach a child discipline if they don't know how to let loose on the football pitch or go wild at their birthday party. In the same way, I would like to ask you to remember the "principle of balance": despite self-control being the cognitive ability which is perhaps most able to predict academic and social success, one of its greatest virtues lies precisely in knowing when to apply it, and when not to apply it.

You can help your child understand it if you reinforce their self-control in situations where you consider it appropriate to have it. Logically, their behaviour will not be the same when you are at a picnic in the countryside as when you are out for dinner in a restaurant. Exposing the child to different people, contexts and situations and always explaining what rules they must obey, can help them to understand the different degrees of self-control that they must display at any given moment. You can also help them to know how to lose control by giving them free rein when they are allowed it. Giving them free rein does not mean explaining to the child what they can and cannot do; it simply means allowing them to act freely without feeling your presence or approval. When you notice them being self-conscious, you can encourage them to "act silly" or "go crazy", to take as many sweets as they want or to get angry if they feel like it; but above all, you should help their mirror neurons, those capable of reflecting your behaviours in their brain, by letting your hair down and enjoying yourself when you think the situation requires it. When one of my children hears me say: "Crazy time!", they immediately go into "fun mode" because they know that their father is going to break a rule and enjoy himself to the full.

Remember

Self-control is the ability to know how to master frustration, postpone satisfaction and learn how to order our actions to achieve our goals. Help your child to tolerate frustration, cultivate their patience, carefully plan how they are going to solve a problem or think about the future can help them master self-control. An effective strategy for achieving this is to establish clear limits and create moments when the child can enjoy themselves, free from rules.

25

Creativity

> All children are born artists, the problem is how to remain an artist as we grow up.
>
> (Pablo Picasso (paraphrase))

Neuroscientists passionately believe that the real treasure of the human mind is its ability to adapt and solve new problems. Both skills depend heavily on creativity. We could say that imagination and inventiveness belong to children, yet this creative capacity could be compared to the survival of the panda or mountain gorilla. With each year that passes without us protecting them, these species will come closer to extinction. This is neither speculation nor a sentimentalist point of view. Numerous studies show that creativity, unlike other cognitive functions, peaks in childhood and is lost as the child grows. Precisely for this reason, this chapter will not be used to explain the child's creative capacity; instead I am going to try and explain to you how you can help them to conserve it, to be able to enjoy it throughout their life.

Recently, neuropsychologists have become interested in the phenomenon of "divergent thinking". These two peculiar words define our ability to see alternatives. In a classic test of divergent thinking, a person is given a brick and is told to think about all the things it could be used for. An adult is usually able to give an average of fifteen uses before running out of ideas. Highly creative people are able to reel off about two hundred. Divergent thinking is not synonymous with creativity, but it is a very important intellectual capacity when it comes to being creative. Creativity is much more important in our lives than we tend to think. Any person – in life, at work, in social or emotional relationships – needs a good creative capacity. In fact, nowadays creativity is the basis of our definition of intelligence: "The ability to solve new problems". In this sense, a person may be very efficient and perform their duties diligently, but not very creative or intelligent when it comes to solving new issues. Nowadays, many parents, teachers and companies encourage the first model of thinking over the second. However, this educational model is likely to take away opportunities for our children. As Einstein explained: "Logic can take you from A to B. Imagination can take you everywhere".

DOI: 10.4324/9781003360117-30

Sir Ken Robinson, possibly one of the most enthusiastic advocates of new education systems, has a theory about why this happens. Current educational systems were devised during the time of the Industrial Revolution, and therefore designed to educate our children in a manner similar to the way cars are assembled in a factory. Different teachers pull different strings with one main objective in mind: that the child increases his or her performance or efficiency when performing tasks. In this model, the main focus is on getting adults to be more productive and to adjust to standards, but not necessarily more creative or adaptable when facing life. There is a study that provides good proof of this, and which will give all parents something to think about. In it, a series of tests were carried out on a range of adults and children in order to assess their capacity for divergent thinking and to give creative solutions to new and old problems and situations. They were shown objects, such as a wheel or a clip, and were asked to indicate as many uses as they could think of for those objects. They were also asked to give as many ideas as possible in order to solve social and material problems. As expected, adults gave the most appropriate answers, but their scores were lower in quantity and originality than those of children. What is really surprising is that the final score of preschool children was almost fifty times higher than that of the adults. It is a huge amount. No adult could run fifty times faster than a five-year-old child. Nor can adults learn fifty times more words in an hour, reel off fifty times more animals in a minute or have a vocabulary that is fifty times richer than a child of that age. If we were lucky, the comparison could be double, or triple the amount, but no – children are actually fifty times more imaginative than adults.

Going from 98 per cent to 2 per cent is a great achievement for parents and educators. How can you have such an innate ability to fade away? The answer is that more than just fading away, it is an actual burial.

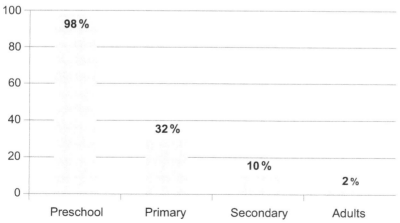

Source: Land, George, and Jarman, Beth, *Breakpoint and beyond: Mastering the Future – Today* (HarperBusiness, 1993).

I am of the opinion – and I make this known in my lectures on creativity – that we are all tremendously creative. We only need to go to sleep to unleash our wildest imaginations. The difference between a brain that is asleep and a brain that is awake is that the limits, regulations and fear of censorship are largely dissipated. Children's brains are more creative than those of adults, because that great filter of censorship – norms and social conveniences – has not yet been incorporated. A child can draw a dragon on the north pole, add an astronaut cat and then his brother as a porcupine without ever coming up against the barrier of prohibition. Their imagination can soar way above any inhibitions or burdens. However, as we become adults, our frontal lobe incorporates a whole series of norms, regulations, rules, schemes, ideals, archetypes, prototypes and models that extinguish or bury that creative spontaneity that we enjoy so much when our children are small.

However, the child's brain development is not solely responsible for this creative decline. Parents, educators, schools, colleges and "education" systems also have a large share of the responsibility. Throughout their childhood, every child has to endure an infinite chain of corrections, improvements, criticisms, disapprovals, approvals, reproaches, mutterings and condemnations that make being creative too inconvenient and painful. When we say to a child: "You have done very well", this reinforces the idea that acting appropriately is positive, without going beyond expectations. When we say something such as "What fun!", "What a great idea!", to a child who is showing that they are thinking outside the box, we are reinforcing their imagination.

There was an interesting study that asked a series of teachers how important it was for them that their students were creative. Every one of them said it was very important. However, when these teachers were asked to order the different qualities of their students – obedience, intelligence, discipline, tidiness, attention, comradeship, etc. – in order of importance, they all placed creativity last. Perhaps at home parents also prioritise other skills over creativity. In my opinion, I think we should make an effort at home and at school to relax the rules, change expectations regarding our children and provide a space for creativity, so they can express themselves in everyday life. This morning my five- year-old son took apart the inhaler that the doctor had just prescribed for a bronchial problem. When I went into the kitchen, just in time to take him to school before going to work, I was surprised to see the six-piece inhaler was splayed across the table. A question immediately came to my mind: "What's with all this mess?". It is probably what my parents would have said to me. However, perhaps because I was in the middle of writing this chapter, I reconsidered what I wanted to say just in time and instead said to him, "Are you investigating?". Looking at me happily he said: "Yes". I told him: "Knowing how things work and wanting to take them apart is a sign of intelligence. But we're going to leave it here because we are in a hurry. We can put it back together later". Instead of leaving home frustrated and angry about the inhaler experiment, we left home beaming from ear to ear. And what's more, we arrived on time.

Comments that "kill" creativity. Avoid saying ...	Comments that preserve creativity. Try saying ...
"That's not how you do it."	"What fun!"
"That's not right."	"Great idea."
"You've made a mistake".	"Will you show me?"
"Try and do it again properly."	"That's so cool!"
"I'm going to show you."	"I love it."
"You've done it the wrong way around."	"I really like how you've done that."
"It's wrong."	"Did you come up with that yourself? You've thought about it very carefully."

As you can see, there are comments that kill creativity and others that preserve it. In the same way, there are also attitudes and strategies that help your child retain their creative potential. Here you can read the ones that experts consider the most important.

Give them tools to express their creativity

Every creative person is surrounded by tools that help them express themselves, be it a film camera, paintbrushes or a typewriter. A child also needs tools that allow him or her to express themselves. Offer them a place to create, where they have sheets of paper and coloured pencils, plasticine, Lego® or construction pieces. You can also provide a dressing-up box for your children. You never know when they will want to dress up and create stories and characters. The important thing is for the child to have the tools available to express their creative side.

Offer them freedom

In their choice of games, their choice of reading topics, or subjects to draw or write about, freedom must be a priority. I am sure that you have your informed opinions about why it is more interesting for your child to draw a horse instead of an ogre, however, we know that the true way for your child to find their own inspiration is for them to draw and play with what they really want. A few chapters ago we talked about Nancie Atwell, the winner of the Global Teacher Prize who managed to get her students to read forty books a year, and who lets them choose the ones they like the most. It turns out that Atwell also gets her students to write more, and to a higher standard, than in other schools; the secret of her success relies on her wisdom to let the child write on whichever subject he or she chooses, every time. As you can see, offering the child freedom so that they can improve their desire to learn and express themselves is primarily a matter of trust.

This is perhaps the main advantage of educational models that offer a greater degree of freedom to the child or engage with their enthusiasm;

models such as project-based learning. In this type of model there is a syllabus, as in all educational programmes, but the child has greater freedom to search for their own sources, gather information and create their own "textbook" with all the information that the child and their classmates have been able to find. In addition to this, each child can handle different parts of the project based on their interests, rather than following a uniform learning programme. Without a doubt, introducing creativity and a curriculum that is focused on the interests of the child into the academic calendar, is a great advantage for learning according to what we understand nowadays about the brain and how it learns and develops.

Give them time to get bored

Boredom is the mother of all creativity. All the greatest creative geniuses came up with something during a moment of boredom. When the child has nothing to do and does not have anything to occupy their time, their brain begins to get bored and seeks, via their imagination, new ways to be entertained. If there is no boredom, if the child is glued to the television or if their day is filled with extracurricular activities, their creativity will be drowned out by a lack of opportunities to express themselves. The child who has everything and who does not have time to get bored seldom grows up to be a creative person.

Show a creative attitude

Remember that you are a model for your children. Use creativity on a daily basis. Do not always cook the same thing, dare to innovate and create in the kitchen. Be creative when you help them do their homework and use all your imagination when you play together. You can invent your own tales and stories instead of always reading stories written by others. You can ask them to offer creative solutions when you have to solve a domestic problem, such as running out of milk, or what you can eat when there is no bread left to make sandwiches. In my house it is one of our favourite games. The children fall about laughing, inventing crazy solutions such as dipping a muffin into shower gel or making a sandwich by cutting a carrot in half lengthways. They will definitely come up with many great ideas and you will have a great time doing it. When they are older, this ability to think up crazy ideas will allow them to find good, practical solutions to any problem that arises throughout their lives.

Place emphasis on the process, not the result

Often, parents help their child in their school art projects and strive to make it amazing. However, to help your child retain their creativity, the important thing is not to be able to draw well, to know all the answers or to solve the problem correctly, but to use their imagination to think.

Throughout their life this skill will be as important as all the others put together. You can observe them while they are drawing, constructing something or inventing a game and ask yourself: are they having fun doing it?, do they come up with interesting ideas?, have they managed to translate their ideas into something real, be it a game, a drawing or a construction? If so, their imagination has been reinforced because they will have had a very rewarding experience.

Don't interfere

If there is an area in which not interfering is more important than doing so in order to develop their confidence, it is creativity. The creative process means that the child can move freely through their own world. All creativity experts agree that the less parents intervene, the better. It is also important not to reinforce too much. You can tell the child if you like or dislike something, you can make them see that you understand what they wanted to do, but avoid describing their "works of art" or "accomplishments" with words like "good" or "bad". Remember that the important thing is the process, not the result.

Next, we will see how two parents go against creativity using two completely different styles. Daniel's mother is going to put all her effort into making the drawing beautiful. Sarah's mother is going to look on quietly as her daughter draws and then she will discuss the drawing with her.

Help them to connect

One of the characteristics of creative people is that they are able to connect ideas that to others may seem unconnected. Mixing trendy colours with a photograph of Marilyn Monroe, as Andy Warhol did, combining minced meat with a piece of bread to create a hamburger or putting two engines together instead of one to make a plane to transport people are examples of impossible connections that have turned out well. Every day children come up with hundreds of unconnected ideas that parents sometimes try to correct. The boy who discovers naughty words might begin to call people things like "gorilla in a nappy", "Mr. Poo-head" or "a beetle with nits". Some parents rush to correct the child, explaining that they shouldn't say these things, or that the beetles cannot get nits because they do not have hair. As you just saw in the example of the snail with fangs, children's ideas are so original that sometimes adults don't know how to appreciate their true value. I urge you not only to enjoy their world, but also to help them to connect things that are distant from each other. If your daughter wears a striped raincoat, you can ask her what other things have stripes. She can

Interfering in their creativity	Respecting the creative process
M: Daniel, will you show me what you are drawing?	S: Look mummy! Look what I've drawn!
D: Yes.	M: I was watching you draw! You were concentrating very hard!
M: What is it? A snail?	S: Yes, but look what I've drawn!
D: Yes.	M: Wow! What a wonderful drawing!
M: It's very good, but his tentacles are missing.	S: Yes!
D: I was going to draw them on now.	M: It's a snail, isn't?
M: Look, the snail has tentacles and eyes, adding up to four. There are four of them in total.	S: Yes.
	M: And what that's coming out of his mouth?
D: OK.	S: Fangs!
M: And it has a tail coming out the back. See? Let me help you.	M: Goodness me! He must be a dangerous snail!
D: OK.	S: Yes, he's a vampire snail!
M: Oh, and what about drawing a lettuce leaf? Snails love lettuce.	M: So scary!
	S: Yes, and there's a flying worm too.
D: How do you do that?	M: You're right! Look at those wings.
M: Look, like this, in green. I'll draw it for you.	S: Yes, they're for flying!
D: ...	M: I love it. Will you give it to me? I'm going to put it next to my bed. Although I might be too frightened
M: Doesn't it look good?!	...
D: I'm going to play. I don't want to draw anymore.	S: Yes!! I'm going to draw something else.

tell you that a zebra, a pedestrian crossing or a prisoner's pyjamas all have stripes. Letting out a small roar may also help her to connect stripes with tigers. It may seem like a silly game, but the ability to jump from a striped raincoat to a zebra or a sailor's top is one of the key characteristics of the most creative and intelligent people.

Remember

Creativity is a very important capability for anyone to have. Your child is a master of creativity. Help them maintain it. Limit their timetables, take them away from the television and give them time to get bored and explore new ways to have fun with their imagination. Reinforce a creative attitude and be an example to them. You can give them spaces, moments and tools to develop their imagination, but respect their creative moments above all, so that you avoid directing or rewarding the quality of the result. Do not forget that your child's imagination can take them anywhere they want to go.

The best apps for children under six years of age

My kids will have computers, of course. But they will have books first.

(Bill Gates)

DOI: 10.4324/9781003360117-31

Farewell

It is easier to build strong children than to repair broken men.

(Frederick Douglass)

Many readers are surprised to see that the previous chapter has been left blank. We have received dozens of emails to our publisher asking if it is a printing error, and we have even had negative ratings on websites for not having duly completed the chapter. However, after many editions, I still maintain that it will stay completely blank. As we discussed in the chapter dedicated to attention, the use of apps can cause the child to lose interest in other activities that are much more beneficial to their development. In addition, studies indicate that children who spend more time in front of screens are more likely to develop ADD, behavioural problems or child-hood depression. It is also well documented that for some children these devices can provoke addictive behaviours and create a dependence on them. Screens should indeed feature in the child's life, since they are part of our lives, but in my opinion it is better that they find their way into the child's hands gradually. This should happen once their brain has developed a little more, emotionally speaking, and also improved its ability to control itself. In other words, from the age of six.

Now this has been cleared up, I can tell you that we are now at the end of the book. Talking about children is always an opportunity to have fun with and connect with our inner child. I hope that you will be able to assimilate everything you have read here using your own values and common sense. Remember the principle of balance and apply it with good judgement. The last thing I want is for any parent to cling to every single word I have written and make it sacred. I firmly believe, and have tried to convey, that the key to success in the education of your child is to leave behind entrenched methods and dogmas and to live in the moment. From my experience, a great parent or educator is not someone who follows an entrenched method or one who adheres to an established plan, but one who knows how to detect a child's needs at all times and take advantage of the educational opportunities

DOI: 10.4324/9781003360117-32

offered in our day to day lives. Let's look at a practical example. A few chapters ago I spoke enthusiastically about the importance of instilling a love for reading in my children before going to sleep. However, if you are too tired one day to read your child a story, and they are insistently asking you to do so, explain with sincerity how tired you are. Your assertive response will provide a model for developing their own assertiveness and will help them to develop empathy, placing themselves in the shoes of their tired parent. In addition, they will have to make an effort to conquer their frustration. Your child's brain is like a sponge; it will grasp every opportunity to learn and reach its full development. I encourage you to take advantage of your circumstances to realise your full potential as an educator.

We have immersed ourselves in some of the issues that I consider most relevant in the intellectual and emotional development of every child. Words like "confidence", "responsibility", "assertiveness" or "self-control" may sound too grown-up for such young children. In truth, with a play- and communication-based focus between parent and child, solid foundations on which the child can build their wonderful mind can be built from early childhood. For me, other words such as "extra-curricular activities", "homework", "punishment" or "mobile phones" sound too harsh for a brain that needs to play and develop without pressure, fear or at a frantic pace. In this sense, it is very possible that the most important job of every parent during this time is not to hinder, accelerate or alter the natural development of the brain of their child.

Many of the ideas that you have been able to learn here are not new. More than fifty years of psychological research and educational experience reveal that the fathers and mothers who are the happiest with the job they have carried out, those who have raised children who turn into autonomous adults, with good academic, intellectual, emotional and social development, are not the ones who take their children to the most expensive schools or fill their days with extracurricular activities. The secrets to a successful education are much simpler, although they may require a greater level of personal commitment. These parents are affectionate and create a secure bond with their children. They encourage their autonomy and help them to overcome their worries and their fears. They set clear standards and often reinforce positive behaviour. They also support them in academic and intellectual development. Children observe everything we do, therefore the ability of parents to interact with others also influences the development of their own children. Fathers and mothers who show they have a good relationship with their partner, and are respectful, offering support and showing mutual appreciation, and also those who demonstrate the ability to conquer their frustration and manage stress, are in general a better influence on the emotional and intellectual development of the child. As you have seen, they are simple ideas that every parent can apply if they can show values of respect and understanding towards the child, other adults and themselves, and if they spend the necessary time with their children. Without a doubt, the most important thing for your child and their brain is that you are there.

Neuroscience also tells us that enriching our parent/child conversations, cultivating patience and self-control and fostering emotional intelligence are valid, sensible strategies. What I have tried to capture in this book, and what I personally believe, is that one of the smartest strategies that we can use as educators, and that few parents and educators actually use, is that of helping our children to strengthen the connections that bring together the emotional brain and the rational brain. Using empathy, helping to integrate highly emotional experiences, teaching the child to listen to both their reason and their emotion when making decisions and helping their frontal lobe to exercise self-control when the situation requires it, enriches the dialogue between emotional and rational intelligence. Only when this dialogue is fluid and balanced does true maturity appear; the ability to harmonise our feelings, thoughts and actions in order for them to go in the same direction.

We have arrived at the end of our journey and I want to thank you, from the bottom of my heart, for allowing me to travel with you on it. In this book I have aimed to convey all my knowledge and experiences as a father, neuropsychologist and psychotherapist. It is knowledge that I have learnt and inherited from people who know much more than I do and who have done much more research than I have done. I also wanted to share all the intuitive knowledge and experience that my wife has transmitted to me, especially the importance of playing, of affection, of generosity and of physical contact in the child's education. I feel that half of this book belongs to her. The truth is that you will not have read one single suggestion that I myself do not believe in, because everything I have told you features in my daily interaction with my children. I can assure you that I put all my energy into this short book, but even so, I could never have imagined that I was going to be able to reach so many children and families in so many different parts of the world, after so many editions and translations of the book. That is why I must thank all those who, in one way or another, share with others what they have learnt from this book and their thoughts on it; whether with your brother- or sister-in-law, friends from nursery or the park. I want to thank all those who have lent it to others, given it as a present or recommended it in parenting classes and to those who leave their opinions in the bookshop or on the website where they purchased it. I am so grateful to you. They are gestures of generosity that ensure the message from *Understanding Your Child's Brain* reaches many more children. For me it is a great joy and a great honour to know that this little book continues to help many parents feel calmer and safer in how they educate their children, so they can grow up with less shouting, less anger and with a richer, closer and more positive interaction with their parents.

I bid you farewell by inviting you, once again, to connect with your inner child. Remember that the child's brain is not programmed to perceive or learn in the same way as yours; therefore, the best way to positively influence their development is to get into the world of your child. Get down to their level and play, play, play with them. Enjoy!

Index

Note: *Italic* page numbers refer to figures.

acquired fears 100, 101
action neurons 35
agitation: avoiding 152; signs of 150
American Academy of Pediatrics 126–127
amygdala 89–91
anger: frustration and 43–44; managing 47–48; outburst of 68; parent's 35–36; punishment and 59; regulating 64; upsets and 31
anxiety 43, 92, 97, 103, 108
apps, mobile: attention and 123–124, 126–127; for children under six years of age 163; and video games 148–149
assertiveness: being 104–106; defined 103; giving voice to silent child 108–110; rights, respecting and asserting 106–108
attachment: hormone 83; importance of 85; secure 38; *see also* bonds
attention 121; allowing to let off steam 127; calm 128; until end 129; focusing on positive 113–114; interruptions, avoiding 128; slow 124; spending time with children 127; value of 125–127; wide 123–124
attention deficit disorder (ADD) 65, 125, 127
attitude, for setting limits 66
Atwell, Nancie 142, 159

Baby Einstein programme 4
balance: common sense, educating 25–26; emotional brain and rational brain 24–25; principle of 154, 164
behaviourism 11

Bonaparte, Napoleon 130
bonds 81–83; attachment hormone 83; defined 81; detachment 85–86; making feel valued 86–87; needs of children, taking care of 84; physical contact 84–85; reciprocal conversations, creating 85; secure environment, creating 83–84
de Bono, Edward 144
boredom, creativity and 160
brain development 1–5; communication 72–76; emotional intelligence 79–115; empathy 38–45; establishing limits without drama 64–71; fundamentals of 9–26; intellectual brain, strengthening 119–166; patience and understanding 31–37; principles for 9; punishment, alternatives to 57–63; reinforcing rules and positive behaviour 46–56; tools for supporting 29–76; *see also* emotional brain
Brown, Les 57
Bryson, Tina 109
building, play at 147

calm 2–3, 23, 35–45, 84; attention 128; common sense of 25; confidence and 89–90; feeling of 66; self-control and 152; setting limits 68; traumatic situation and 98–99
censorship 158
cerebral cortex 19
Cervantes 72
de Clapiers, Luc 79
classic building block game 147
collaborative communication 73

common sense, educating 25–26
communication 72–73; -based focus
165; collaboration 74–75; cooperative
73–74; freedom to 75; questioning 73;
thinking and 75; turning tasks into
teamwork 74
concentration 123, 124, 129; *see also*
attention
"conduct-based" distortion of
education 49
confidence 88–89; depriving child
of 89–92; emotional 38; feelings
and decisions, validating 94–95;
genetic component and 88;
positive messages, offering 92–93;
responsibility 93–94
connection, brain 18–19
construction games 147
conversation: positive–elaborative
conversation style 132–135; reciprocal
85; *see also* communication
cooperative communication 73–74;
asking for collaboration 74–75;
freedom to 75; thinking and 75;
turning tasks into teamwork 74
corpus striatum 125
creativity 156–159; ability to connect
ideas 161–162; giving time to get
bored 160; not interfering 161;
offering freedom to 159–160; placing
emphasis on process 160–161; showing
creative attitude to 160; tools to
expressing 159
Cuddle-a-saurus 85

da Vinci, Leonardo 119
decision-making process 25, 94–95
depression, childhood 111–112
desires 11, 32–33, 35, 37, 110, 125
dinner time, patience and understanding
during 33–34
dissatisfaction 57, 112; mutual 60;
reinforcements and 55
distress 26, 36, 64, 93, 113, 152
distrust 86
divergent thinking 156, 157
dopamine 50
Douglass, Frederick 164

Eakins, Thomas 29
eating, strategies for 33–34
Einstein, Albert 31, 72, 137, 156–157

emotional brain 21, 22, 24–25, 40, 85,
94–95, 119; calm and 90; control of
151; corpus striatum 125; development
of 80, 82; importance of 79; parts of
89; region of 41
emotional education 41–42
emotional intelligence: assertiveness
103–110; bonds 81–87; confidence
88–95; fear, without 96–102;
happiness, seeds for 111–115; impact
on 38; teaching 79–80; vocabulary of
feelings and 139
empathy 4, 38–39; defined 39–40;
developing 165; educating with 41–44;
practising 44–45; reasons for working
40–41; using 166
enjoyment: child's development and 17;
parenthood 14–16
euphoria 42
excitement 35, 83, 125
executive intelligence 151–152

faces, making 149
facial expression, emotion and
145–146
Farooq, Raheel 9
far-reaching memories 134
fear 39, 43, 47, 90–91, 165; acquired
100, 101; calming down 96, 98,
102; of censorship 158; facing
100–102; growing up without 96;
instinctive 100; irrational 97; limits
on 89; overcoming 40, 109; traumatic
experiences, assimilating 96–100; to
trust, stages of 101; types of 100
feelings: right to 106; validating 94–95;
see also specific aspects/types
Fivush, Robyn 73
foods 125; preventing problems with
33–34; as rewards 52; take care of 84
Franklin, Benjamin 18
freedom: attention and 127; to
cooperative communication 75;
creativity and 159–160; self-control
and 152, 154–155
Freud, Sigmund 96
frontal lobe 89
frustration 3, 35, 43–44, 55, 165;
facing 64; level of 69; managing
48; overcoming 62, 108, 152; over-
excitation due to 41; patience,
practising 113; tolerating 111, 112, 151

fulfilment, avoiding 112–113
future, self-control of 153–154

Gates, Bill 126, 163
goal achievement, punishment and
    60–61
Goleman, Daniel 80
grammar 141, 142
gratitude, cultivating 114
grief 42
group therapy 108

happiness 111–112; attention on positive
    113–114; frustration, tolerating 112;
    fulfilling, avoiding 112–113; gratitude,
    cultivating 114; patience, practising 113;
    rewarding activities, enjoying 114–115
Harlow, Harry 81–82
Hart, Betty 139
hierarchy of needs, Maslow's 11–12
Hill, W. E. 16
hippocampus 58, 59

images, thinking in form of 144–145
imagination 156; boredom and 160; of
    parents 160; reinforcing 158, 161; *see
    also* creativity
imitation 47
Industrial Revolution 157
inhibitory neurons 35
instinctive fears 100
instructions, playing with 140–141
insula 41, 85–86
"integrating traumatic experience
    process" 97, *97*
intellectual development 119–122;
    attention 123–129; creativity 156–162;
    language 137–143; memory 130–136;
    neuroscience and 126; self-control
    150–155; visual intelligence 144–149
intelligence: concept of 121; definition
    of 156; executive 151–152; quotient
    120–121; sign of 80; social 145, 149;
    see also emotional intelligence
interfering, creativity 161, 162
interruptions, avoiding 128
intuition, brain 19–20
Inuit parents 25, 119
irrational fear 97

jigsaw puzzles 147, 153
Jobs, Steve 126

journeys 31–33
joy 1, 42, 43, 53, 166

Kipling, Rudyard 130

language 121, 137–139; expanding
    sentences 141–142; love of reading,
    instilling 142–143; play with
    instructions 140–141; speaking 139;
    universe, expanding 139–140
Lao Tse 150
learning without mistakes 61
left hemisphere of brain 19–20, 138
Lego® 145, 147, 159
limits 64–65; always 68; attitude for
    setting 66; before 68; calmly 68–69;
    consistently 68; early 68; for living
    together 70; with love 69; rules for
    setting 68–69; time to start setting
    66–68; with trust 69; types of 69–71;
    unbreakable rules 70; for wellbeing 70
logical thinking 144
loss of self-control 154–155
love 43, 52, 65, 68, 125; developing 88;
    hormone of 83; of reading 142–143,
    165; and safety 84; setting limits
    with 69
lunch time, patience and understanding
    during 33–34
lying 61–62, 86, 143

making amends 62–63
Mandela, Nelson 24
maps, making 148
Maslow, Abraham 10, 11
Maslow's hierarchy of needs 11–12
Mayo Clinic 126–127
memory 121, 130–131; defined 133;
    narrating child's life 131; negative 135;
    organization 132–133; photographic
    133; positive 134–135; positive–
    elaborative conversation style,
    developing 132–135; reaching 133–134
men, communication with children 139
middle way *see* balance
mindfulness 128
mirror neurons 47, 104, 154
Mischel, Walter 150
mistakes: and dangers, remembering
    135; learning without 61; right to
    make 107
mobile apps *see* apps, mobile

Monroe, Marilyn 161
Montessori, Maria 1, 16
Montessori method 49
Mother Teresa 103
motivation 60, 120, 125; confidence and
    93; controlling 50
Mozart, music of 4
My Wife and My Mother-in Law (Hill)
    15–16

narratives 131; *see also* story telling
needs: hierarchy of 11–12; taking care
    of 84
negative memories 135
neuroscience 4, 70–71, 126, 166
newborns, protection of 10
New York Times, The 126

organization, of memory 132–133
oxytocin 83, 84–85, 143

parenthood, enjoying 14–16
patience and understanding 31; dinner
    time 33–34; journey home from
    supermarket 31–33; perfect storm
    35–37; practising 113
Pediatrics (journal) 26
personal growth 41–42
photographic memory 133
physical contact 17, 83, 166; avoiding
    losing 84–85; looking for 84–85;
    necessity of 26
Picasso, Pablo 156
Pinker, Steven 11
PISA report 142
placidity 43, 67
Plato 46
playing: -based focus 165; at building
    147; with instructions 140–141; at
    making faces 149; at making maps 148
pleasant emotions 21, 42
positive behaviour, reinforcing 49–50
positive–elaborative conversation style
    132; defined memory 133; memory
    organization 132–133; negative
    memory 135; photographic memory
    133; positive memory 134–135;
    reaching 133–134
positive memory 134–135
positive messages, confidence and
    92–93
positive models of conduct 47–49

positive psychology 112
precuneus memory 134–135
prefrontal cortex 64, 65
present, self-control of 152–153
primitive brain 22
principle of balance 154, 164
psychoanalysis 11
psychology 11
psychotropic drugs, influence of 2–3
punishment 57; achieving goals and
    60–61; aim of 60–61; consequences of
    57–59, 61–62; making amends 62–63;
    reasons for not working 57–59; reward
    and 62; trick-punishments 59–60

rational brain 21, 22, 24–25, 40
rational intelligence 80
reaching memory 133–134
reading, love of 142–143, 165
reciprocal conversations, creating 85
Reese, Elaine 73, 132
reinforcement: dissatisfaction and
    55; guilt and 55; immediate 53–54;
    necessity 53; obligation and 55;
    positive 60; positive behaviour 49–50;
    positive models of conduct 47–49;
    time to 53–55; trick-reinforcement
    55–56; ways to 50–53
relaxation, wide attention and 123
remembering *see* memory
reptilian brain 21, 22
respecting, creativity 162
responsibility, confidence and 93–94
revolutionary theory 111
rewarding 51–55, 62, 92–93; activities,
    enjoying 114–115; controlling future
    154; creativity 161; effective 51; food
    52; ineffective 51; material 51–52;
    punishments and 62; social 52; *see also*
    reinforcement
right hemisphere of brain 19–20
rights 106–108
Risley, Todd 139
Robinson, Ken 157
Roosevelt 88
routines: for creating secure environment
    83–84; for sleeping 26
rules 67–68; classroom 127; establishing
    61–62, 151; free from 3, 152, 155;
    game 128; house-hold 152, 154–155;
    language 138, 141; limits 64–71;
    reinforcing 46–47, 49, 52; social 66

sadness 41, 42, 43–44, 55, 141
satisfaction 43, 49–50, 58, 125, 153; confidence and 53; of having achieved 93; of having got what children wanted 66; obeying rule and 62; reinforcements and 55
secure attachment 38
self-awareness 22, 41
self-concept 58, 59
self-confidence 87; *see also* confidence
self-control 121, 127, 150–151; executive intelligence 151–152; frustration, overcoming 152; of future 153–154; losing 154–155; of present 152–153
self-esteem 12, 45–46, 49, 81, 88, 92
self-fulfilment 11
Seligman, Martin 111–112
Shakespeare 72
shaming 35–36, 100
Siegel, Daniel 109
slow attention 124
smartphones: attention and 126; emergence of 4; tablets and 105, 120, 126, 149
social intelligence 145, 149
spatial function 144
spatial relationships 144, 147
spatial thinking 148
speech development 139
spending time with children 127
story telling 85, 106, 133, 143; bedtime 61–62, 75, 114; about confidence 91; language and 143; memory and 131; reading 68, 114, 128, 165
striatum nucleus 125–126
success, right to 107
sympathy 39, 40
synapses 18

tablets/smartphones 105, 120, 124, 126
Tai Chi, wide attention and 123
tantrums 35–37, 41, 44

television 9, 68, 84, 148, 160; attention and 124, 126, 127; schedules for watching 152; turning off 51, 73, 86, 128
Temple, William 72
thank you, saying 114
Thoreau, Henry David 38
tiredness 14, 43; love of reading and 143; signs of 108
Todos a la cama (Plataforma Editorial) 26
traumatic experiences, assimilating 96–100
trick-punishments 59–60
trick-reinforcement 55–56
trust 12, 40, 53, 86, 145, 159; in ability 113; acting on 91; bond of 82–83, 85; fear to 101; importance of 13; mutual 9, 68, 73; self 86, 95; setting limits with 69
Twain, Mark 88

understanding, patience and *see* patience and understanding
unpleasant emotions 42

video games 105; attention and 124, 125–126; visual intelligence and 148–149
Virgil 14
visual intelligence 121, 144–147, 148–149
visual language 147
vocabulary *see* language
voice giving, to silent child 108–110

Warhol, Andy 161
Wendte, Charles W. 123
Whole-Brain Child, The (Siegel, Bryson) 109
wide attention 123–124
women, communication with children 139
words, thinking in form of 144–145

yoga, wide attention and 123

Taylor & Francis eBooks

www.taylorfrancis.com

A single destination for eBooks from Taylor & Francis
with increased functionality and an improved user
experience to meet the needs of our customers.

90,000+ eBooks of award-winning academic content in
Humanities, Social Science, Science, Technology, Engineering,
and Medical written by a global network of editors and authors.

TAYLOR & FRANCIS EBOOKS OFFERS:

A streamlined
experience for
our library
customers

A single point
of discovery
for all of our
eBook content

Improved
search and
discovery of
content at both
book and
chapter level

REQUEST A FREE TRIAL
support@taylorfrancis.com